The First
British Workmen's
Compensation Act, 1897

by David G. Hanes

An almost inevitable consequence of the Industrial Revolution was the growing demand in the late nineteenth century for a law providing compensation for workers injured at their jobs. A number of individual suits against employers met with mixed success; the employer's legal resources were usually superior to the worker's, and litigation was costly. The need for a generally applicable law had become pressing by the end of the century.

A law results from the actions of legislators, and the figures associated with the Workmen's Compensation Act included some of England's most prominent statesmen: Herbert Asquith, then a young man rapidly advancing in the government; former prime minister William Gladstone; and Joseph Chamberlain, known earlier as a champion of the worker's welfare. The author draws upon their political backgrounds and the educational and social influences that shaped them to explain the position taken by each.

Mr. Hanes has skillfully mined the relevant documents in the British Public Record Office, documents not previously exploited, to put together an absorbing and concise account of the reasons for and tactics of the passage of the 1897 Act—a milestone in British social legislation. Yale College Series, 8.

Mr. Hanes, a 1966 graduate of Yale College, is attending Columbia Law School.

THE FIRST BRITISH WORKMEN'S
COMPENSATION ACT, 1897

THE FIRST BRITISH

WORKMEN'S COMPENSATION ACT

1897

by David G. Hanes

New Haven and London, Yale University Press, 1968

K

Library of Congress catalog card number: 68–27755

Designed by John O. C. McCrillis,
set in Garamond type,
and printed in the United States of America by
The Carl Purington Rollins Printing-Office of
the Yale University Press, New Haven, Connecticut.

Distributed in Great Britain, Europe, Asia, and
Africa by Yale University Press Ltd., London; in
Canada by McGill University Press, Montreal; and
in Latin America by Centro Interamericano de Libros
Académicos, Mexico City.

TO ANN

Yale College Series

The tradition of undergraduate writing and publishing has long been a very lively one at Yale, as witnessed by the large number of periodicals, journalistic or literary in character, which have appeared on the Yale campus. These, however, fail to give an accurate picture of the high proportion of good and original scholarly writing which is also done by undergraduates. The excellence of many of the Honors theses written by Yale Seniors made it desirable some years ago to give the most deserving of them the circulation which publication in printed form could provide. Between 1941 and 1957 ten volumes were published in the Undergraduate Prize Essays Series and two in the Scholars of the House Series. The authors of several of these essays have gone on to fulfill amply the promise of their early scholarly efforts. More recently the growing number of theses of outstanding merit has encouraged Yale College and the Yale University Press to establish this new YALE COLLEGE SERIES with the hope that every year it will be possible to publish some of the best work by the Honors majors in the Senior Class. The selection, which is necessarily a very rigorous one, was performed for the Class of 1966 by a faculty committee made up of Messrs. M. I. J. Griffin, David Calleo, and E. M. Waith, Chairman.

GEORGES MAY
Dean of Yale College

Acknowledgments

I would like to express my gratitude to the men at the Public Record Office in London for their many kindnesses in directing my researches to the proper files. In addition, they very kindly permitted me to make photocopies of the documents cited in the text; the photocopies are on file at the Yale Law School library.

To Professor Robert Stevens of the Yale Law School, who suggested the topic and made time in his busy schedule to direct my research and to suggest alterations in the manuscript, go my warmest thanks. Also I want particularly to thank Professor David Calleo, who courageously waded through the first draft and suggested areas where rewriting was needed, and my wife, who has been a saint about proofreading and retyping and to whom this volume is dedicated.

Finally, I should say that, while this book has benefited greatly from the kind assistance of those mentioned above, such mistakes of fact or interpretation as may yet be found are entirely my own.

D. G. H.

January 1968
Millbrook, N.Y.

Contents

Acknowledgments   ix

Introduction   1

1. Common Law Remedies   5

2. Employers' Liability Act of 1880   15

3. Preparations for the Future   26

4. Personalities: Gladstone and Asquith   42

5. Employers' Liability Bill of 1893   57

6. Workmen's Compensation Act of 1897   87

Appendix I. Employers' Liability Act, 1880   109

Appendix II. Resolutions Concerning Contracting Out
Received at the Home Office   114

Bibliography   115

Index   119

Introduction

Nineteenth-century England witnessed the beginnings of modern industry. Since the size and complexity of such industry required investment capital beyond the means of all but a few entrepreneurs, the industrialists of the nineteenth century resorted to the joint-stock company, which rapidly replaced the small capitalist employer. These gave way to boards of directors. The resultant impersonal nature of industry has been blamed for the tension and ill feeling between employer and employed. Certainly the helplessness of the individual worker in the face of his employer's overwhelming economic strength accounts for the rapid growth of trade unionism toward the end of the century: only through massive organizations could the worker hope to bargain on equal terms with the new management.

In their early days the labor unions concerned themselves first of all with survival, and then with securing higher wages for their members. For this reason their direct influence in promoting the Workmen's Compensation Act was minimal: the most that may be said for them is that they did not oppose it. In the same way, they had not been responsible for the Factory Acts, the sanitation laws, or the laws regulating age and working hours of women and children, though to be sure they had welcomed these new laws. Later, in the twentieth century, they would be the initiators of social reform, but not yet. In the nineteenth century the cause of the working class still depended upon a few enlightened and courageous individuals drawn from the aristocracy and the middle class. The battles over reform legislation were bitter, for the entrenched middle class generally controlled the bulk of the House of Commons, and only the most severe pressure could induce them to moderate their notions about laissez-faire and freedom of contract.

In 1897 the British Parliament passed the Workmen's Compensation Act. With slight modifications the principle embodied in that bill remained unchanged for fifty years; during that time the bill provided workmen with their main source of compensation for injury or death suffered in the course of their employment.

When the Conservatives introduced the bill into the House of Commons in the spring of 1897, both its friends and its foes described it as the most important and revolutionary piece of legislation in the nineteenth century. Yet scarcely a single voice spoke out against it in the House of Commons, and the House of Lords passed the bill's third reading by a vote of 69 to 6. Sir James Joicey, a wealthy coal owner who voted for the bill, announced in the House of Commons that there was "more socialism pure and simple in the Bill" than in any bill submitted in the last half-century. Why was such a bill introduced by a Conservative Government? Why did it receive so little opposition? Why has it to this day attracted so little attention?

The answers to these questions lie in what happened before 1897. The Conservatives introduced the bill because they had pledged themselves to do so. The bill faced little opposition because the battle had already been fought and won overwhelmingly in an earlier engagement. And the bill attracted little attention at the time because its passage was a foregone conclusion and the people, bored with the debate, had focused their interests elsewhere.

The events leading up to 1897 form the subject of this book. In the case of the common law the events must necessarily span the century, for most decisions are grounded on the authority of precedent. As to the personalities directly involved in introducing, supporting, or opposing the legislation, the impact of earlier events in their lives must be considered. For events directly influencing the legislation itself, one need look no further than the attitudes of the people, the campaign promises of politicians, and the election returns.

The principal events do not center around the passage of the Workmen's Compensation Act; as this book will show, that had to happen. Rather they concern the events leading up to the failure of the Employers' Liability Bill of 1893, for out of that failure grew the events of 1897.

CHAPTER 1

Common Law Remedies

For my part neither sneers nor abuse, nor opposition, shall induce
me to accept as the will of the Almighty and the unalterable dis-
pensation of His providence a state of things under which millions
lead sordid, hopeless and monotonous lives without pleasure in
the present and without prospect for the future.

JOSEPH CHAMBERLAIN
Glasgow, 15 September 1885

While the Factory Acts sought to prevent accidents by enforcing
supposedly safe operating procedures, the incidence of industrial
accidents remained fairly constant throughout the nineteenth century. Today a certain number of industrial accidents per year are
accepted as inevitable: unforeseeable failures of men and equip-
ment occur at a predictable rate. In the nineteenth century, legislators still labored under the delusion that all accidents could be
prevented if only the proper precautions could be prescribed and
enforced. But as the century drew to a close, with thousands still
killed or maimed annually, accident prevention gave way to compensation for the victims. The last serious attempt to legislate
accident prevention occurred in the Employers' Liability Bill of
1893. By making the employer fully liable for all the negligence
of his employees, Parliament sought to induce management to
take all possible precautions against accidents. That theory was
successfully discredited, and four years later the Workmen's Compensation Act granted, as a first charge on the cost of production,
the right to compensation for injury to all workmen.

Before 1897 the injured worker found himself in severe difficulty. The remedies at his disposal were few, inadequate, and

uncertain. Today he may resort to National Health Service for his medical treatment, state-administered Workmen's Compensation while incapacitated, and Unemployment Insurance to tide him over between jobs. Then he was dependent upon charity or such insurance as he had been able to secure for himself. In rare circumstances, and if the worker was enterprising, the common law or the Employers' Liability Act of 1880 might offer relief. Of the latter more will be said later. The common law, as an instrument of relief, was altogether inadequate and fraught with difficulties; had it not been so, there would have been no need for the step eventually taken.

When Victoria came to the throne, the extension of civil liability (as opposed to criminal liability) to its present state had barely begun; but the principles upon which civil liability rested had already begun that rapid expansion and transformation which characterize the nineteenth century as one of the most dynamic in the history of the law. It was, of course, recognized that civil suits were intended to remedy personal wrongs arising out of another's acts or omissions. In the late eighteenth century, Blackstone had differentiated such personal actions into those founded on contracts (a set of promises agreed upon by the parties to the contract, for breach of which there are legal remedies), and those founded upon torts (failure in a duty imposed by law irrespective of consent). Blackstone had relegated negligence to the status of an anomalous exception in the middle of a chapter on "implied contracts."[1]

Today negligence stands as the single largest heading under the general classification of torts. If the phrase "tortious act" means anything at all to a layman, it means a negligent act; and the magic word "negligence" conjures visions of successful lawsuits and substantial awards. But in the very early nineteenth century that does not appear to have been the case. Negligence, as an action all by itself, had barely begun to be recognized; instead it existed as an

1. Sir William Blackstone, *Commentaries on the Laws of England*, ed. W. D. Davis (4 vols. Philadelphia, Rees Walsh, 1902), 3, 163.

element in other actions such as, for instance, trespass on the case, nuisance, and, occasionally, contract.[2] For a large part of what we would today call negligence actions, negligence as it is now understood played no part at all. Such actions fell under the heading of trespass. To recover in trespass, the plaintiff had only to show that he had been injured by the direct action of the defendant. Although the history is still debated, apparently negligence, intent, or other wrongful conduct played no part at all: proof of direct action leading to the injury seems to have been enough in trespass.

In the limited sense described, liability for a trespass has been compared to the strict liability theories that lie at the bottom of a growing portion of tort law today. Whether the analogy is valid is best considered elsewhere[3]; but whatever the merits of the contention, English judges on the crest of the industrial revolution recoiled in horror from the implications of liability without fault —implicit in the law of trespass—for the owners of industry. Instead, the manifest tendency of the judges was to limit recoveries in trespass actions by adding the requirement of negligence.[4] In actions sounding in contract they followed Blackstone's lead by refusing recovery for negligently inflicted harm unless the harm occurred within the bounds of the contract: that is to say, unless one of the terms (express or implied) of the contract declared that the defendant owed the victim a duty to be careful, the victim could not recover for negligently inflicted harm.

Whatever the procedural niceties, negligence always carries with it some onus of culpability, some implication of a failure which, while not criminal, is sufficient to impose liability. But, aside from the early trespass action just discussed, civil liability includes another and well-established class of cases that impose liability without any direct imputation of fault whatsoever: such,

2. Winfield, *"The History of Negligence in the Law of Torts,"* 42 *Law Quarterly Review* 184, 195–97 (1926).
3. See generally Harper and James, 2 *Torts* 747–52 (1956).
4. Gregory, *"Trespass to Negligence to Absolute Liability,"* 37 *Virginia Law Review* 359, 362–65 (1951).

among others, are the cases which grow out of the relation of master and servant. Long before the beginning of the nineteenth century an employer, in addition to his own personal behavior, was held responsible for the tortious acts of his servants if their acts were committed, as the ironic phrase goes, within the scope of their employment. In practice this last condition has given rise to much contention, but when it is held to have been complied with, then the master is deemed to be as liable for his servants' acts as if he had committed them himself. The principle is called vicarious liability. Until 1862 it seems to have been at least an open question whether, if the tortious act were committed in disobedience to the master's instructions, such disobedience might not disallow redress. But in that year Justices Willes and Blackburn decided in the case of *Limpus v. London General Omnibus Company* that such disobedience was irrelevant: "The law is not so futile as to allow the masters, by giving secret instructions to the servant, to set aside their liability."[5] At the same time Willes and Blackburn insisted that not only must the servant have been acting within the scope of his employment, but also his intention at the time the act was committed must have been to further the master's interests. With only one other exception, to be considered below, the master's liability was absolute.

Various attempts to explain the above rule of vicarious liability by the maxims *"Respondeat superior"* and *"Qui facit per alium facit per se"* were made, but, as Baty points out, these are not explanations but merely Latin statements of a rule of English law.[6] On what then is the rule of vicarious liability founded? Not on the blameworthiness of the master, for patently he is not to blame; nor on the master's control over the servant, for he is held liable even if the servant is acting contrary to the master's instructions; nor on the ground that the master selected the servant who did the injury, for the master selects his contractor but is not liable

5. C. H. S. Fifoot, *Judge and Jurist in the Reign of Victoria* (London, Stevens and Sons, 1949), p. 46.
6. Thomas Baty, *Vicarious Liability* (Oxford, Clarendon Press, 1916), p. 9.

for the contractor's negligence. Oliver Wendell Holmes has suggested that the origin of this doctrine goes back to Roman times when the servant, a slave, was the chattel of the master; under such circumstances retribution was exacted upon the offending chattel, thereby indirectly occasioning a loss to the master. Later, Holmes argued, the master was permitted to pay damages directly to the victim, rather than suffer the same loss by the mutilation or death of his servant.[7]

Another view suggests that it has its origin in a mistaken parallel between innkeepers (the classic example of liability without personal fault) and ordinary masters, i.e. the invitation of an innkeeper to the public to repose trust in the safety of his premises and servants involves that innkeeper in liability for such safety; the mistake lies in supposing that a similar invitation to trust, as exists between innkeeper and public, exists between the master of a servant and a passing or casual third party. No such invitation, it is argued, does in fact exist.

Throughout the nineteenth century the origin and justice of the rule of vicarious liability were bitterly contested. At least as late as 1916 feeling still ran strongly on the subject: in that year Baty wrote angrily, "You clothe a factor with credit, and he may involve you up to the hilt of that credit. But if you clothe a coachman with livery he may involve you in damages without any limit whatever."[8] But most nineteenth-century writers agreed, if only by implication, that the law of vicarious liability was grounded in public policy; that the real reason for the employer's liability was that the damages were taken from a deep pocket instead of from the original tortfeasor, in all probability a man of straw. Occasionally a judge was strong enough to tell the truth: Mr. Justice Willes, in *Limpus v. London General Omnibus Co.*, said, "There should be some person capable of paying damages and who may be sued

7. Oliver Wendell Holmes, Jr., *The Common Law* (Boston, Little, Brown, n.d.), pp. 8–15.
8. Baty, p. 13.

by people who are injured."[9] By the last half of the nineteenth century, therefore, a master, like anyone else, was civilly responsible for his own personal negligence, the suit for which might be grounded either in the independent tort of negligence, in trespass, or in personal failure to fulfill a duty of care agreed upon in contract. In addition the law had made an important stride in developing the rule of vicarious liability. But once confronted with an action for negligence, an employer had at his disposal three basic and powerful defenses: first, no negligence but unavoidable accident; next, *Volenti non fit injuria:* the plaintiff voluntarily encountered the risk and therefore has no action; third, contributory negligence on the part of the plaintiff (while the employer admits his own negligence, if he can prove that the plaintiff was at least partially responsible for causing the accident the plaintiff will be barred from recovery). Also it should be remembered that the difficult burden of proving negligence always lies with the plaintiff.

If the plaintiff happened to be a worker the risks and pitfalls confronting him were enormous. In the first place, he had the odious task of proving that the man upon whom his future livelihood probably depended had been negligent in the conduct of his business. Having undertaken to run that risk, he next had to choose the correct form of action and plead it properly—for an error at this stage could easily cause dismissal of his claim. Finally, he had to establish negligence against whatever defense the employer might raise, and the difficulties he probably would encounter in securing evidence might easily be insurmountable. Supposing that he won, the amount awarded to him would hardly seem worth the trouble, for the extravagant, punitive awards common today were unknown to the Victorians.

In the above situation it is supposed that the worker was injured because of the direct, personal negligence of his employer. Under the impersonal conditions outlined in the Introduction, the employer might never set foot on the premises nor exercise any direct

9. Fifoot, p. 46.

control over the mechanics of production at all. Under such conditions the question of his direct personal negligence could never arise. If the negligence lay with the foreman or a fellow employee, it would not be worth the victim's while to sue them, for costs would eat up whatever pittance could be extracted.

In the last described case of injury caused by a fellow servant, one alternative remaining to the injured worker was to sue his master, relying on the rule of vicarious liability. Here the common law deserted him completely: against such an action the employer had at his disposal the defense of common employment. Whereas, by the rule of vicarious liability, the master may be liable to a third party for the negligent acts of his servants, the doctrine of common employment held that such an action will not lie if the victim is a fellow servant with the actual tortfeasor, i.e. if the two share a common employer.

The doctrine of common employment seems to have had its origin in the case of *Priestley v. Fowler,* decided in 1837. A butcher's boy sued his master for injury which he had suffered through the breakdown of his master's cart. The cart broke because it had been overloaded. When the overloading was proved to be due to the negligence of a fellow servant, the judge barred the butcher's boy from recovery. The case was decided by Lord Abinger who wrote,

> Where should we stop? We should have a master liable to his servant for the negligence of the chambermaid in putting him into a damp bed; for the negligence of the upholsterer in sending in a crazy bedstead, whereby he was made to fall whilst asleep; for the negligence of the cook in not properly cleaning the saucepans; for that of the butcher in sending in bad meat; and for that of the builder who, by putting in bad foundations, caused the house to fall, and bury master and servant together.[10]

10. A. H. Ruegg, *The Laws Regulating the Relation of Employer and Workman in England* (London, William Clowes and Sons, 1905), p. 137.

In view of such excited language and Lord Abinger's failure to cite any authority for his opinion, it has been argued that the above decision is an instance of judge-made law amounting to a clear departure from common law rules. If this is true, the departure was made on public policy grounds in order to avoid the imposition of a crippling liability on the still young industrial revolution, in much the same way that negligence was added as an element in the ancient tort of trespass. Professor Levy has even gone so far as to accuse Lord Abinger of being a politically prejudiced judge who allowed party considerations to affect his judicial decisions.[11] However that may be, clearly the doctrine of common employment aimed at curtailing the rule of vicarious liability at least as far as it extended to the master's own servants. The doctrine remained a rule of common law until the Labor Government abolished it altogether in the Law Reform (Personal Injuries) Act of 1948.[12]

Whatever its sources, from its inception the doctrine of common employment has been the subject of bitter controversy. The arguments in support of it are usually of this kind: there is no reason to suppose that the doctrine arose from any class prejudice in favor of the employer; rather it was based upon what appeared to the judges to be the reason and equity of the case. The question at issue is whether constructively there has been a breach of obligation on the part of the employer toward the person injured. When the victim is a stranger, it is clear that he has done nothing to disentitle him to redress. But when the victim is a servant of the employer, injured by a fellow servant, a new element has been introduced: the victim is not a stranger for he is under a contract of service to the employer. Does the contract of service render the employer liable to one servant for the negligence of another? In the absence of express terms, does the contract include implied terms to that effect? Clearly it does not if, for instance, employer and employed

11. Sir Arnold Wilson and Hermann Levy, *Workmen's Compensation* (2 vols. London, Oxford University Press, 1939), *1*, 25, n. 2.

12. It should be noted, however, that owing to several strong decisions in the 1930s the rule had by that time become a dead letter anyway.

are viewed as engaged in a common enterprise run for the mutual benefit of both.

The more usual argument views the contract of service from the other end: in interpreting the contract of service the law sees an undertaking on the part of the servant to accept the risks incident to the service. One of those risks is the negligence of fellow servants. When a man is injured by such negligence the rule of *Volenti non fit injuria* will bar him from recovery.[13]

Lord Bramwell, a vigorous opponent of vicarious liability in any form, justified the doctrine of common employment in yet a third way by saying that there was no such thing. The common law, he argued, holds a man accountable only for his own personal acts or defaults; vicarious liability was an exception to this rule, and the doctrine of common employment merely reaffirmed the basic rule of the common law. Since the contract of service already included (in wages) remuneration for any risks run in the course of employment, the worker could expect no further compensation in the event of injury.[14]

On the other hand, the objections made to the doctrine usually include the following: the doctrine of common employment is a modern, anomalous, judge-made exception to the general rule of vicarious liability. It is founded on an implied contract, which is a legal fiction bearing no relation to the facts. When, in addition to what is expressed in a contract, there is something else in the contemplation of both parties which they would have expressed had either party required it, then the law is entitled to say that such a contract must be taken to have been entered into. Such a condition, if it involves the cession of enormous rights without any consideration, is altogether iniquitous and sure to be wholly unknown to the person alleged to be bound by it. In addition it is argued that the doctrine has been pushed to extreme lengths by judges who force and twist the meaning of "fellow servant" until the employer's

13. Ruegg, p. 138.
14. Charles Fairfield, *A Memoir of Lord Bramwell* (London, Macmillan, 1898), p. 349.

responsibility has reached a vanishing point: the general manager
of a railway company is now held to be in common employment
with a plate-layer employed on the line.[15] The iniquity of the
situation is further apparent in the case of a very small employer,
who both works with his employees and directs them, for he will
be liable in any case of injury arising under his supervision attributable to his negligence; the employer of thousands of employees,
who delegates authority, is rendered effectively immune. By declaring that managers are fellow-servants with the laboring men
in a mine, a factory, or a workshop, the law offers a premium on
the delegation of all power from the master to his subordinates,
since he is thereby relieved from the liability which he had while
he managed his own affairs. That thereby the recipients of such
authority themselves become liable is irrelevant, for by their position in life it is not worthwhile to sue them. In short the courts
have, by an imaginary contract, restricted the claim for compensation to fellow servants who are unable to pay.

15. Ruegg, p. 139.

CHAPTER 2

Employers' Liability Act of 1880

Whatever justifications or objections may have existed in the minds of lawyers, the workmen of England were united in opposition to the doctrine of common employment. As far as they were concerned, it discriminated against them by putting them in a worse position vis-à-vis their employers than any stranger. Such understanding as they had derived either from the passionate harangues of popular leaders, or from the hard experience of being denied recovery in an action for personal injuries; feeling accordingly ran high on the subject, and by the 1870s it had become a bone of political contention.

Quite predictably, the protest against the doctrine of common employment was first raised in Parliament by one of labor's principal spokesmen, Mr. Alexander Macdonald. His bill of 1876 proposed the total abolition of the defense, and also of the defense of *Volenti non fit injuria.* He withdrew his bill on the understanding that the Government (Disraeli's last) would inquire into the matter by means of a Select Committee. In the same year, and again in the following year (1877) a Select Committee of the House of Commons was duly appointed,

> To inquire whether it may be expedient to render masters liable for injuries occasioned to their servants by the negligent acts of certificated managers of collieries, managers, foremen, and others to whom the general control and superintendence of workshops and works is committed, and whether the term 'Common Employment' could be defined by Legislative Enactment more clearly than it is by the law as it at present stands.[1]

1. Public Record Office (PRO), Home Office (H.O.) 45/9865/B13816/123.

After hearing much important legal testimony, the majority of the committee were in favor of a minuscule reduction of the scope of the doctrine of Common Employment:

> Your Committee are of opinion that in such cases as these, that is, where the actual employers cannot personally discharge the duties of masters, or where they deliberately abdicate their functions and delegate them to agents, the acts or defaults of the agents who thus discharge the duties and fulfill the functions of masters should be considered as the personal acts or defaults of the principals and employers, and should impose the same liability on such principals and employers as they would have been subject to had they been acting personally in the conduct of their business.[2]

Insofar, in other words, as the agents represented the alter ego of the principals, the latter were to be held liable. Mr. Lowe (later Lord Sherbrooke) presided over the committee and submitted his own report. In it he recommended

> that the funds of every industrial undertaking shall be liable to compensate any person employed in such undertaking for any injury he may receive by reason of the negligence of any person exercising authority mediately or immediately derived from the owners of such undertaking, with this qualification, that the liability to indemnify shall not extend to persons who, though exercising authority, are *bona fide* employed in actual labour as distinguished from superintendence.[3]

Thus, Mr. Lowe would have abolished the defense of common employment in the case of any workman exercising authority, however low in the scale he might be, so long as he was not employed in actual labor.

2. PRO, H.O. 45/9865/B13816/123/App. I, para. 12.
3. Ibid., App. II, para. 15.

About the same time (June 1877) the Royal Commission on Railways turned in its report; it was greeted with considerable enthusiasm, for railway accidents provided spectacular examples of the glaring inequalities of the law: whereas hundreds of passengers obtained remuneration for injuries suffered as the result of a train wreck, the firemen, brakemen, and conductors, similarly injured and equally innocent of negligence, could expect none from their employers. The report suggested that the law be changed to place railway servants in as nearly the same position in respect of railway accidents as would "be consistent with the principles of the law of master and servant."

> The servants . . . assert that in numerous cases they are sacrificed from causes and in circumstances which would clearly give a right to compensation were it not that the law refuses to regard in any other light than as their fellow servants those to whom the companies delegate the master's authority.[4]

The report went on to develop the position that the rule of law whereby a master is responsible for the acts of his servants is based upon the presumption that he directs and controls their conduct. In fact, the report acknowledged, such is seldom the case and the fiction is only maintained on the ground of public policy in the interests of third parties. Accordingly the Royal Commission recommended that railway companies should be made liable to their servants for the negligence of those to whom the master's authority is delegated; a railway company should not by reason of its acting altogether by deputy avoid the liabilities which the law intended to impose upon a master toward his servants.

In the storm of controversy which followed, Macdonald re-introduced his bill for total abolition of common employment and Sir R. A. Cross (Home Secretary) pledged the Government to deal with the subject. Little seems to have come from that

4. Ibid., App. III.

pledge, perhaps because of a confidential Memorandum drawn up
by the Attorney-General, Sir John Holker, and printed for the
private use of the Cabinet on 27 November 1878. It reads in part:

> The true conclusion to be drawn from the long investigation
> of this matter seems to be—
>
> 1. That the law, which makes an employer liable for the
> negligent acts of his servants committed in the course of their
> employment, is in principle indefensible.
>
> 2. That the exception, by which the employer is exempt
> from the liability if the injured person and the person guilty
> of the negligence causing the injury are fellow-servants, is
> also indefensible.
>
> We have thus to deal with an unjust exception to a bad law.
> The obvious remedy is to alter the law so as to render no
> exception admissible, enacting that employers shall not be
> liable to anybody for the negligent acts of their servants.
> This would put an end to the grievance which is based upon
> inequality of treatment . . . If adopted the law will be founded
> upon an intelligible and a sound principle.[5]

Whatever the effect of the above rather astonishing document,
Disraeli's Government did manage to draw up a bill on the more
moderate lines adopted by the majority of the Select Committee
in their recommendations. The bill was never discussed in Parliament in the year of its introduction; the following year (1880)
the Lord Chancellor reintroduced it in the House of Lords, which
in turn referred it to a Select Committee. Before the committee
could hold its second sitting Parliament dissolved, a general election was called, and Disraeli's Government went out.[6]

Not for the last time did employers' liability become a campaign issue. Until the question was finally settled nearly twenty
years later, it reemerged in each general election and in every by-
election held in worker-dominated constituencies. The victorious

Liberals in the election of 1880 had made campaign promises to abolish the doctrine of common employment. To live up to those promises was one of their first tasks. But Gladstone's Government did not introduce a new measure on the subject; pressed for time, they introduced Mr. Brassey's bill of 1879. This time it was put forward as a Government bill and bore the names of Mr. Dodson (President of the Local Government Board), Mr. Joseph Chamberlain (President of the Board of Trade), the Attorney-General (Sir Henry James), and Mr. Brassey. Mr. Brassey's original bill had been a rather muddleheaded compromise, and so the new bill remained even after systematic revision in committee. The Fourth Party, as the young Tory coterie under the leadership of Lord Randolph Churchill was known, surprised the Liberals by its violent but reasoned attacks alleging that the bill did not go nearly far enough in the workman's favor. The Fourth Party objected most of all to the exclusion of domestics—"merely because they had no votes."[7] After an extremely prolonged discussion the Commons passed the Bill; at the instance of Lord Beaconsfield,[8] the House of Lord's amended it to expire after two years, which term was subsequently extended to seven years by a compromise with the House of Commons.

The Act, as passed, was intended to be a temporary compromise measure. Gladstone's Government, pressed for legislation to fill their campaign promises, adopted a private member's bill. The legislation

> had not originated in the great departments of the State and was, both in principle and in drafting, an amateurish suggestion which might, indeed, sound very plausible and accommodating; but which had not been clearly thought out in a scientific spirit with the advantages of official information.[9]

7. Winston S. Churchill, *Lord Randolph Churchill* (2 vols. New York, Macmillan, 1906), *1*, 140.
8. Disraeli went to the House of Lords as the Earl of Beaconsfield in 1877.
9. Churchill, *1*, 136.

It did not abolish the doctrine of common employment; it merely removed it as a possible defense in five specified cases or sets of circumstances. In somewhat condensed form the bill reads as follows:

> The workman, or in case the injury results in death, the legal representatives of the workman, and any persons entitled in case of death, shall have the same right of compensation and remedies against the employer as if the workman had not been a workman of, nor in the service of the employer, nor engaged in his work, where personal injury is caused to the workman in the following cases:
>
> 1. By reason of any defect in the condition of the ways, works, machinery, or plant connected with or used in the business of the employer; provided (section 2[1]) that the defect therein mentioned arose from or had not been discovered or remedied owing to the negligence of the employer, or of the person in the service of the employer, and entrusted by him with the duty of seeing the ways, works, etc. were in proper condition.
>
> 2. By reason of the negligence of any person in the service of the employer who has any superintendence entrusted to him whilst in the exercise of such superintendence. [Section 8 limits the term superintendent to one whose sole or principal duty is that of superintendence, and who is not ordinarily engaged in manual labor.]
>
> 3. By reason of the negligence of any person in the service of the employer, to whose orders or directions the workman at the time of the injury was bound to conform, and did conform, where such injury resulted from his having so conformed;
>
> 4. By reason of the act or omission of any person in the service of the employer done or made in obedience to particular instructions, given by any person delegated with the authority of the employer in that behalf, provided (Section

2[2]) the injury resulted from some impropriety or defect in the rules or bye-laws, or instructions therein mentioned; and where a rule or bye-law has been approved, or has been accepted as a proper rule or bye-law by one of Her Majesty's Principal Secretaries of State, or by the Board of Trade, or any other Department of the Government under or by virtue of any Act of Parliament, it shall not be deemed for the purposes of this Act to be an improper or defective rule or bye-law;

5. By reason of the negligence of any person in the service of the employers who has the charge or control of any signal, points, locomotive engine, or train upon a railway.[10]

In brief, the Act curtailed the defense of common employment in five cases where the workman suffered injury owing to the negligence of persons who, here, may be conveniently labeled foremen. But in order to bring a case within the act, it was necessary to prove that its circumstances corresponded with one of the five above, and owing to the vagaries of the language this often proved very difficult. For example, the provisions state that the workman shall have the same remedy as if he were not a workman in the employer's service; these words do something more than merely remove the defense of common employment: they put the workman in a new position, and the standard of due care that may be demanded of an employer varies according as the person concerned is a stranger, a servant, a person invited, etc. What is the plaintiff's new position?

Section 2(3) of the Act (see Appendix I) has been interpreted by the courts to be a qualification of the defense of *Volenti non fit injuria* to this extent, that whatever may have been the case under the common law, in suits under the 1880 Act mere continuance of the servant in the employer's service with full knowledge of the danger is no longer necessarily to be considered sufficient to establish that he has voluntarily undertaken the risk. This was decided

10. See App. 1.

in the case of *Smith v. Charles Baker and Sons,* on appeal to the
House of Lords in 1891.[11]

Finally, while the Employer's Liability Act of 1880, both in
intention and in fact, extended the employer's legal liability beyond
the limits thus far imposed by the common law, at the same time it
placed limits on the amount recoverable under its provisions. The
limit was fixed at the estimated earnings of the victim during
the three years preceding the injury; the limit was to be computed by inference from the known earnings of a person similarly
placed during those years in a like employment in the same district.
Other than this relative scale, no upper or lower limits were set.

Long before the Workmen's Compensation Act of 1897 passed
into law, British working men had taken steps to solve the problem
of compensation for injuries arising out of their employment. By
contributing a certain sum to a worker's pool they gradually built
up their own compensation insurance funds. As the funds grew
larger their management became a full-time job; reaching the
stature of autonomous organizations, they became known by the
generic name of Friendly Societies. These societies provided financial remuneration to the worker or his dependents in case of
disability or death; such financial assistance was given irrespective
of any considerations of negligence on the part of either the worker,
his foreman, or the employer. The only consideration was that the
worker should be a contributing member of the fund at the time
of his accident. By 1880 the Friendly Societies were a firmly established feature in the lives of many workers in diverse fields.

Prior to 1880 employers do not seem to have been in the habit
of contributing to these workmen's insurance funds, although such
contributions were by no means unheard of. For instance, in the
coal mines of the Lancashire and Cheshire districts, it was a condition of service imposed by the masters that the miners should
belong to a Friendly Society which insured them against all manner
of accidents.[12] The masters agreed to contribute 15 per cent of

11. (1891) A.C. 325.
12. PRO, H.O. 45/9865/B13816/123, p. 54.

the contribution of each man. But the big impetus to the societies came with the passage of the Employers' Liability Act of 1880. Many employers, uncertain as to the extent of their increased liability under the new law, offered to make sizable contributions to the workers' insurance funds. In consideration for their contribution, they required the workers to forgo their rights to institute suits for damages. The practice described was known as "contracting out," and it instantly became a source of serious contention. Lucid, reasoned, well-supported and entirely contradictory claims appeared in support of both sides.

The principal arguments against the practice of contracting out are as follows: (1) If workers are allowed as a matter of public policy to contract out, there is no guarantee, because of the inequality of bargaining power, that they may not be induced to contract out for the mere consideration of being employed, whereupon the workman finds himself in worse condition than if the bill had never been passed. (2) The Act in some sense represents the workman's charter by putting him in the same legal position toward his employer as any casual third party; he should not be able to forgo such rights. (3) The threat of litigation with all its attendant horrors of public exposure and possible cost tends to make the employer more careful and responsible; whenever contracting out occurs, the employer, no longer threatened, tends to negligence and the incidence of accidents goes up.[13]

On the other side, the arguments in favor of the practice of contracting out run as follows: (1) When workers are injured and have contracted out, their case is taken care of expeditiously, generously, and automatically, without recourse to the courts; this fosters a spirit of cooperation rather than contenion. (2) To prohibit the practice of contracting out would cause the employer to withdraw his contribution to the insurance funds; this contribution generally far exceeds the actual cost of his liabilities at law, and accordingly the employer appears as a benefactor rather than an

13. Ibid., p. 23.

enemy out of whom compensation can be squeezed only with the utmost difficulty; furthermore, these funds pay compensation in cases where recourse to a law suit would not avail the victim, e.g. when the injury was occasioned by the man's own negligence, or by no negligence at all but accident. (3) To prohibit contracting out manifestly interfered with the freedom of the individual to dispose of his property as he sees fit. (It should be noted in passing that this particular argument cuts both ways: those in favor of prohibiting contracting out also argue that to give up the right to seek reparations puts the worker in a position of weakness from which he cannot exercise any future influence over his employer at all; that the whole object of the law in the first place is to put the worker in the same free and untrammeled position as the rest of the world; and therefore that it is no interference with the individual's freedom to guarantee that he does not lose it.)[14]

The legality of such a contract was immediately challenged in the courts and upheld by the decision in *Griffiths vs. Earl of Dudley,* where the Queen's Bench declared it legal for a workman to contract out of the Act with his employer by covenanting for a consideration not to claim compensation for personal injuries under the Employers' Liability Act.[15] Since it was unclear precisely what the worker was giving up by such a contract, it was equally uncertain what constituted adequate consideration.

As has been said, the usual consideration for contracting out was a contribution by the employer to the worker's insurance fund. Such contributions generally amounted to a sum equivalent to from 15 to 25 per cent of the worker's contribution. In effect, then, the worker's benefits from his Friendly Society were increased by as much as one quarter. The question whether such a contract was advantageous revolves around the likelihood of his recovery of damages at law, and the amount of those damages in the event he succeeded. It was notoriously difficult to succeed under the Employers' Liability Act. In 1890, for instance, 389 cases were

14. Ibid.
15. 9 Q.B.D. 357 (1881).

tried under the Employers' Liability Act for a total amount claimed of £63,070. Of these, 208 were successful, but the amount awarded was only £8,679, or approximately forty-one pounds, four shillings, per case in the event of success. These figures are generally typical; the average amount awarded per annum for the twelve-year period 1880–92 was slightly in excess of £8,000.[16]

This figure does not, of course, reflect the whole of the operation of the Act. It does not reflect the cases settled out of court because of a threatened action under the Act; nor does it take account of cases to which the Act could have applied but for the worker contracting out. Least of all does the figure of 389 cases reflect anything approaching the total number of industrial accidents. These considerations should be borne in mind in order to emphasize the essentially trifling consequences of the Employers' Liability Act of 1880. The truth of the matter seems to have been that, as with the common law, litigation under the Act cost more than it generally was worth: the worker, a poor man, found himself in the position of launching a suit against the man upon whom his future livelihood probably depended. Add to this that the legal proof of such negligence was a hazardous matter at best, and it becomes clear why, for the workman, a legal claim for damages only answered in cases of extreme injury. Such cumbersome machinery was unsuited for the more usual injury resulting in temporary disability; for such injuries the Friendly Societies were vastly preferable sources of support.

When the Employers' Liability Act expired in 1887, Parliament extended its operation for another year. By means of such annual extensions Parliament kept the Act in effect until 1948 when the Law Reform (Personal Injuries) Act rendered it a dead letter by abolishing the doctrine of common employment altogether. Between 1880 and 1897, however, Parliament passed no further legislation dealing with the plight of the injured workman. But bills on the subject were introduced almost every year and by 1897 the issue had become one of major political importance.

16. PRO, H.O. 45/9865/B13816/123, p. 18.

CHAPTER 3

Preparations for the Future

"The thirteen months from June, 1885, to June, 1886, are the most complicated in modern British political history."[1] So writes R. J. Evans, and those complications lie beyond the scope of this book. Nevertheless, it is important to understand some of the forces at work insofar as they bear on the question of employers' liability legislation. During that period critical rearrangements of political alliances took place, rearrangements which eventually led to the formation of the immensely powerful Unionist Government of 1895. What the Conservatives gained in political power, the Liberals lost. On the face of it that fact alone explains the failure of the Liberals' Employers' Liability Bill and the enactment of the Conservatives' Workmen's Compensation law: the Liberals did not have the necessary votes to either pass their own Bill or block that of the Conservatives.

In 1885 Gladstone sat at the head of the Liberal party. He had reached the apogee of his personal power and influence and was backed by a solid phalanx of aristocrats who might still be labeled Whigs. Beneath the established older generation of professionals, a rising group of hot-headed and turbulent young men under the leadership of Joseph Chamberlain and Sir Charles Dilke agitated for radical reform. Impatient of the old order, the Radical wing of the Liberal party had anxiously awaited since 1880 the momentarily expected retirement of Gladstone from the party leadership, at which time they expected to decide the struggle between Whig and Radical in favor of a new era of social reform.[2] Around 1883

1. R. J. Evans, *The Victorian Age 1815–1914* (London, Edward Arnold Publishers, 1950), p. 273.
2. J. L. Garvin, *The Life of Joseph Chamberlain* (4 vols. London, Macmillan, 1932), *1*, 312.

Henry George's book, *Progress and Poverty,* had appeared. Among radical workingmen it awakened new imaginings and aspirations, for it eloquently described the glaring contemporary contrasts between the wealth of the few and the distress of the many. Chamberlain read it and was electrified.[3] The dominant theme running through his speeches was, in effect, that after years of waiting the common people were about to enter their own kingdom: social legislation to reform the glaring deficiencies would march through gates thrown wide by extensions of the franchise.

Chamberlain vigorously addressed himself to extending the franchise in the Reform Bill of 1884. In a letter to Gladstone dated 11 December 1883 from the Board of Trade he wrote,

> My own view clearly is that the extension of the franchise and the widening of the basis of our representation will tend to strengthen the Throne, and that the only possible danger to monarchical institutions would be the continued exclusion of the majority of the people from any share in the government.[4]

Chamberlain's support of the measure was so enthusiastic as to lead him to offer to lead a workers' march from Birmingham to London, to which the Marquis of Salisbury replied that if he led such a march he would "return from his adventure with a broken head if nothing worse." Chamberlain hotly retorted by urging Salisbury to lead the opposing array: "In that case if my head is broken it will be broken in very good company," he said.[5] Ten years later the two would lead the Unionist alliance and together head the most powerful Government of the century.

To the horror of the older group of Liberals, Chamberlain began a unilateral campaign of election speeches in 1885 whose content derived pretty much from his own initiative. The speeches of that one-man campaign came to be known as the "Unauthorized Program," and it was specifically aimed at the voters newly en-

3. Ibid., p. 384.
4. Ibid., p. 403.
5. Ibid., p. 467.

franchised by the Reform Bill of 1884, the significance of which Chamberlain was one of the first to grasp. The opening shot of the Unauthorized Program was fired in his famous "Ransom" speech delivered on 5 January 1885. Speaking about the new democracy, he announced the arrival of the millennium:

> Every man was born into the world with natural rights, with a right to share in the great inheritance of the community, with a right to a part of the land of his birth. . . . Private ownership has taken the place of these communal rights, and this system has become so interwoven with our habits and usages, it has become so sanctioned by law and protected by custom, that it might be very difficult and perhaps impossible to reverse it.
>
> But then I ask what ransom will property pay for the security which it enjoys? . . . There is a doctrine in many men's mouths and in a few men's practice that property has obligations as well as rights. I think in the future we shall hear a great deal more about the obligations of property and not so much about its rights.[6]

The "Ransom" speech must not be taken out of context, for his subsequent speeches disallow the interpretation likely to be accorded it by a modern reader. In another speech of the Unauthorized Program, delivered on 29 January in Birmingham, he remarked that indolent and inefficient landlords "must be taught that their ownership is a trust . . . limited by the supreme necessities of the nation."[7] On 5 August in a speech at Hull he further clarified his stand: "It is not our duty, it is not our wish, to pull down and abase the rich, although I do not think that the excessive aggregation of wealth in a few hands is any advantage to anybody; but our object is to raise the general condition of the people."[8]

As if to further compound the horror with which the Glad-

6. Ibid., p. 549.
7. Ibid., p. 556.
8. Ibid., 2, 61.

stonian Liberals regarded their Radical colleague, Chamberlain wrote a highly sympathetic Preface to a collection of articles published during July 1885 in book form under the title, *The Radical Program.*[9] The articles had been running for nearly two years in the *Fortnightly Review,* and the editor's Introduction (not Chamberlain's) ran in part,

> They [the articles] sound the death knell of the laissez-faire system . . . The goal towards which the advance will probably be made at an accelerated pace is that in the direction of which the legislation of the last quarter of a century has been tending—the intervention, in other words, of the State on behalf of the weak against the strong, in the interests of labor against capital, of want and suffering against luxury and ease.[10]

The Unauthorized Program, and Chamberlain's loud announcement that he would join no government not committed to such views, began the contest of wills between the new Radicalism and the old Liberalism, between "construction," and "liberation," between Chamberlain and Gladstone.

At this point a glance at the Irish question is in order, for when Chamberlain finally bolted the Liberal party it was over Home Rule. The election held in November 1885 returned 86 more Liberals than Conservatives, largely owing to the vote-drawing power of Chamberlain's Unauthorized Program. This majority was precisely balanced by Parnell's 86 Irish members, and accordingly any government remained in office only on Parnell's sufferance. Gladstone had become a complete convert to Home Rule sometime during the summer of 1885; when, therefore, the Irish threw the Conservatives out in January, it was inevitable that Gladstone's 1886 Government should introduce a Home Rule Bill. It did so on 8 April and Chamberlain promptly resigned from the Government. He would concede a limited, federal sort of

9. Elsie E. Gulley, *Joseph Chamberlain and English Social Politics* (New York, Columbia University Press, 1926), p. 23.
10. Garvin, 2, 57.

Home Rule but not Irish autonomy, the direction in which Gladstone's measure clearly tended. He intervened with crushing effect in debate against the measure, and when a division was held on the second reading on 8 June, 93 Liberals voted with the majority to down the measure by 343 votes to 313.[11] Gladstone promptly appealed to the country and suffered a smashing defeat: the voters returned 316 Conservatives, 191 Gladstonian Liberals, 85 Parnellites, and 78 Liberal Unionists, as the followers of Chamberlain called themselves. Gladstone resigned and Salisbury formed his second Government.[12]

Excepting only Lords Spencer, Ripon, Rosebery, Kimberley, and Granville, virtually the entire Whig peerage left Gladstone over Home Rule;[13] with them went the great majority of the upper middle class, and of course Chamberlain's personal following as well. Gladstone, at the age of 76, was not impressed; with the single-mindedness of old age he pushed on for Home Rule until his death. Tentatively, anxiously, uneasily, the Liberal Unionists found themselves moving closer to the Conservatives, not on the basis of conviction, but because there was nowhere else to go. Within a few months of the fateful division, Chamberlain understood the consequences:

> Whether the process occupies a generation or a century, 'poor little Wales' must wait until Mr. Parnell is satisfied and Mr. Gladstone's policy adopted. They will not wait alone: thirty-two millions of people must go without much needed legislation because three million are disloyal.[14]

Just so long, he went on to say, as the Gladstonians control the party and commit it to Home Rule, so long will the party be

11. R. C. K. Ensor, *England 1870–1914* (Oxford, Clarendon Press, 1936), p. 99.

12. Evans, p. 279.

13. Philip Magnus, *Gladstone: A Biography* (New York, E. P. Dutton, 1954), p. 395.

14. Garvin, 2, 320.

shattered and reform held up. Chamberlain moved closer to an alliance with both his former Whig opponents and the Tories under Salisbury.[15]

The Conservative party, as well as the Liberal party, was discomfited by the presence of a turbulent and vociferous radical element in the form of the Fourth Party. A. J. Balfour, John Gorst, and Lord Randolph Churchill constituted the nucleus of the coterie, with Churchill the acknowledged leader. In the course of little more than half a dozen years in Parliament, Churchill had bearded and brushed aside everyone who stood in his path. Devastating in debate, he had attacked Gladstone with fearless irreverence; powerful and compelling on the platform, he had captured the Tory caucus from Salisbury (for a time). At the age of thirty-six he became Leader of the House of Commons by driving Sir Stafford Northcote out (causing him to be kicked upstairs to the House of Lords). At thirty-seven Churchill could compel a Cabinet post as Chancellor of the Exchequer from Salisbury by virtue of his personal power in the House and the constituencies.[16]

Salisbury had difficulty in coming to terms with Churchill, who was erratic and a demagogue, and when in December 1886 Churchill foolishly resigned through a miscalculation of political realities, Salisbury made no effort to conceal his satisfaction or to get Churchill back into the fold: "Did you ever know a man who having got rid of a boil on his neck wanted another?" he wrote to a friend.[17] While this may have been a loss to nascent radicalism in the Conservative party, the loss was short-lived for Churchill and the Irish question had already succeeded in directing Chamberlain's footsteps toward the Conservatives. In fact, part of what Salisbury objected to so much in Churchill was the latter's friendship for Chamberlain, "which made him insist that we

15. Gulley, p. 74.
16. J. A. Spender and Cyril Asquith, *Life of Herbert Henry Asquith, Lord Oxford and Asquith* (2 vols. London, Hutchinson, 1935), *I*, 51.
17. Evans, p. 280.

should accept that statesman as our guide for internal politics."[18]

Chamberlain felt himself to be a comrade-in-arms with Churchill, for they had much in common. Both were champions of radical doctrines similar in method and intention, and both were in favor of the Unionist alliance. In a speech at Hackney on 24 July 1885 Chamberlain exclaimed, "Why, this man is doing in the heart of the Tory citadel, with the rarest audacity and courage, the work we have vainly attempted to do from the outside. I am amazed at, and I admire, his courage and his success."[19] The Irish question still dominated party controversy in the year following Churchill's resignation, and the controversy was sufficiently heated to keep the Liberal Unionists bound to the Conservatives even if the alliance was at times uncomfortable for both partners.

Salisbury and Churchill saw eye to eye at least on the Irish question, for both opposed Gladstone's version of Home Rule on the ground of unswerving loyalty to the idea of the unity of the Empire and Great Britain. That Salisbury further opposed Home Rule because he did not want the landholders left to the mercy of an exclusively Irish government need never have been discussed. But their alliance required tactful handling, at least in public, since only months before the two had publicly exchanged what amounted to threats of physical violence. Chamberlain's opponents accused him of apostasy and labeled him "Judas"; the epithet stuck for the rest of his public career. Salisbury likewise frequently found himself in an awkward position because of his Liberal Unionist friends: During the 1892 election campaign he felt compelled to write to Chamberlain urging that the latter tone down his claims that the Conservatives had "come around" to his way of thinking. Such claims, said Salisbury, gave the Conservatives the uncomfortable feeling that they had deserted their colors— a feeling for which there were no grounds.[20] Nonetheless, by the

18. Lady Gwendolen Cecil, *Life of Robert Marquis of Salisbury* (4 vols. London, Hodder and Stoughton, 1921), *3*, 336–37.

19. Garvin, *2*, 590.

20. Ibid., p. 545.

time the 1892 elections arrived, main points of the Unauthorized Program had been passed into law, specifically free primary education and the extension of local government to the counties. Chamberlain was able to write in his personal diary,

> Personally, and on a great variety of subjects, Salisbury, Balfour and W. H. Smith were ready to take as broad and liberal a view as I could wish, but they were sometimes restrained by pressure from some of their followers. On the Church question it was always understood that they would stand firm against any proposal for Disestablishment. . . . During the whole period from 1888 to 1892 there was never any serious difference as to the actual policy of the Government which in the least threatened the existence or the cordiality of the alliance.[21]

In the same way that the politics of the 1880s helped to determine the ultimate alliance during the 1890s, so the proposed legislation on employers' liability during the 1880s formed the groundwork for the legislation proposed by the two parties in the 1890s.

With the passage of the Employers' Liability Act of 1880, Parliament and the country temporarily lost interest in the issue. Admittedly, the 1880 Act was an experiment; and the results would have to be evaluated before anyone could get very aroused over further amendments to the law. But from the very first the labor unions throughout England and the three Liberal-Labor representatives in Parliament (Thomas Burt, Henry Broadhurst, and Alexander Macdonald) announced their settled opposition to one of the bill's most significant side effects: contracting out.

After *Griffiths v. Earl of Dudley*[22] declared the practice not contrary to law or public policy, Burt and Broadhurst annually introduced a bill to amend the situation, until 1886 when they missed a year because of the appointment of a Select Committee

21. Ibid., p. 415.
22. 9 Q.B.D. 357 (1881).

to investigate the operation of the 1880 law.[23] The Liberal-Labor representatives' bills do not seem to have received much notice, although in 1883 the bill got as far as a proposal to read it a second time. It was opposed by the Liberty and Property Defense League whose mouthpiece, Sir J. Pease, moved the following resolution:

> That it is inexpedient to interfere with that freedom of contract between employers and employed, which enables them to contract themselves out of the Act of 1880, and by mutual arrangement and mutual payment to make provision for every workman who may be injured, and the family of every workman who may be killed, whether the accident is one coming under the provisions of the Act of 1880, or is one not so provided for.[24]

The resolution was carried by a majority of 149 to 38. Not daunted, Broadhurst and Burt continued to agitate against contracting out.

As we have seen, the Reform Bill of 1884 transformed England into a real, if still limited, democracy. With the extension of the franchise the total number of voters rose from three million to five million. For the first time the election of 1885 reflected the voices of most of England's miners, and many other hitherto excluded laborers. Chamberlain clearly had grasped the implications, as the speeches of his Unauthorized Program reflect. And when Gladstone formed his Government in February 1886, his choice of Henry Broadhurst for a Cabinet post as President of the Board of Trade indicates that he, too, was not above responding to the pressures from organized labor.

When the inevitable pressure from labor against contracting out resumed, this time Gladstone's Government responded favorably by referring the matter to a Select Committee. Sir Thomas Brassey, a long-time friend to labor, was appointed by the Gov-

23. 1881, Bill no. 71; 1882, Bill no. 57; 1883, Bill no. 33; 1884, Bill no. 35; 1885, Bill no. 61.
24. Parliamentary Debates, Third Series, 280, 514.

ernment to chair the committee. The Members appointed to sit
on the committee were specifically instructed to inquire into the
operation of the Employers' Liability Act of 1880; they did so by
taking extensive evidence from ordinary workmen, members of
trade unions (mostly railway servants and miners), lawyers,
insurance experts, and employers. Their conclusions, and most
especially their recommendations, cast light on the failures of
the Act; in addition the recommendations played a large part in
determining the direction taken by subsequently proposed legislation. It should be borne in mind while considering the latter that
the committee was composed of men favorably disposed toward
labor and genuinely concerned with the welfare of the working-
man.

In its Special Report the committee found that:

> A general concurrence of opinion was expressed as to the
> advantages which the workmen have derived from the ex-
> isting Act. The apprehensions as to its possible results in
> provoking litigation and imposing heavy charges upon em-
> ployers have proved groundless, while a useful stimulus has
> been given to the establishment of provident funds and asso-
> ciations, in many cases liberally supported by the employers.[25]

Their recommendations included a resolution to the effect that no
contract entered into with a workman should bar recovery, under
the Act, of compensation for injury unless upon entering into
such a contract a consideration other than mere employment was
tendered to the workman. Such consideration should include a
contribution by the employer to the workman's insurance fund,
to bear "a full proportion to the contribution" made by the workman himself; and compensation payable to the injured workman
from such a fund was to be "fully adequate, having regard,
amongst other things, to the amounts recoverable as compensation under the Act." Furthermore the employer was to guarantee

25. PRO, H.O. 45/9865/B13816/123, App. V.

any amounts payable by the insurance society in the event, from whatever causes, it failed to meet its obligations. The committee dealt with the problem of the liability of contractors and sub-contractors by recommending that the principal employer be held liable for any injuries to the employees of subcontractors arising out of defects (attributable to the negligence of the principal employer) in the "ways, works, machinery or plant" which is the property of or furnished by the principal employer. Thus liability was not to be entirely escaped by delegating to subcontractors the conduct of the employer's business.

On the subject of amount of compensation to be awarded, the committee recommended that, upon an express finding by either judge or jury that the sum equivalent to three years' wages was inadequate, additional compensation could be awarded by the judge or jury not to exceed a total of £150. Seamen were to be included for accidents arising in home ports; "omnibus and tram-way servants" were to be included in the general extension of the Act to include "all workmen . . . who have entered into or work under a contract of service made with the employer, either verbal or in writing, whether the work be performed in the employer's workshop, or elsewhere, and whether involving manual labor or not."[26]

It may be assumed that each one of the committee's recommendations aimed at curing a specific failure of the Act or a current abuse which ought to be remedied by the Act. Thus we may conjecture that not all employers were liberal in their contributions to workmen's insurance funds; that some took advantage of their workers by making contracting out a precondition of much-needed employment; that some of the Friendly Societies were unable to meet their obligations, thus leaving the injured worker who had contracted out with no remedies whatsoever. Despite these implied criticisms, the committee unanimously agreed that "the operation of the Act of 1880 has been attended with no

26. Ibid.

hardship to the employers, whilst it has been of great benefit to the workmen."[27]

Burt and Broadhurst picked up where they had left off in 1886. Their bills of 1887 and 1888[28] prohibited contracting out in the future, or at any rate declared that no such contract would stand in bar of recovery under the Act. This provision did not affect contracts already made; these were to remain in force although they were not to be renewed. Sections 2(2) of their bill contained a provision that in computing the amount of compensation to be paid to the plaintiff the court was to take into consideration the employer's share of any compensation already paid to the victim out of his insurance fund. Since, at common law, in computing damages no account is to be taken of any money which the plaintiff has received by way of insurance, it may fairly be assumed that Burt and Broadhurst recognized the real value of the employers' contributions to the Friendly Societies and wished, by this provision, to remove any inducement to the employer to discontinue his contributions.[29]

The Burt and Broadhurst bills did not substantially modify the scope of the defense of common employment; the extent of an employer's liability was to remain essentially what it had been since 1880. But in 1891 Mr. Burt introduced an Employers' Liability Bill which abolished the defense of common employment altogether; it is significant that in his bill of that year no contract, past, present, or future, could constitute a defense against an action under the bill.

Salisbury's Conservative Government took no action on the problem of employers' liability until 1888, when Henry Matthews, the Home Secretary, prepared and introduced a bill substantially along the lines suggested by the Select Committee of 1886: omnibus and tramway servants were included if injured owing to the

27. Ibid.
28. Numbers 163 and 71 respectively.
29. PRO, H.O. 45/9865/B13816/123, p. 15.

negligence of those in charge of the vehicles; the principal employer became liable if the employee of a subcontractor was injured
as a result of defective ways, works, machinery, etc., negligently
supplied by the employer; and a seven-paragraph Section 3 defined
the conditions under which contracting out was to be allowed.
Essentially the conditions required that the worker request in
writing such a contract; that the employer contribute an adequate
sum toward the employee's insurance; that, in the event the insurance was not paid when due, the employer undertake to make
good the default; that the benefits of such insurance be equivalent to the compensation recoverable under the Act; that one of
the Principal Secretaries of State in the case of coal mines, metal
mines, factories, or workshops, and the Board of Trade in the case
of any other employment, be the final judge of whether any such
contract was made in pursuance to "adequate" contributions by
the employer.[30]

The Conservative bill, well-intentioned if badly phrased, met
with unrelenting resistance from the labor representatives, who
persisted in opposing any scheme which extended the employer's
liability while at the same time allowing him to "contract out."
The Government did not persevere with the bill even though the
second reading was carried by 202 to 141. In 1890 they again introduced a bill substantially the same as that of 1888. The provisions under which contracting out was to be permitted were
simplified:

> 3. No contract made after the commencement of this Act,
> whereby a workman deprives himself of any right under this
> Act, shall constitute a defense to an action brought for the
> recovery of compensation under this Act, unless it is made in
> pursuance of a . . . substantial consideration which is, in the
> opinion of the Court before which such action is tried, a
> reasonable consideration for the workman so depriving him-

30. Ibid., p. 16.

self of rights under this Act, and is other than the consideration of entering upon . . . the employment.[31]

In other words, the Conservative bill would have shifted the onus of deciding whether a contract was fair or not from the Government to the courts.

The bill, number 172, was introduced on 27 February 1890, published on 28 March, and read for the second time on 14 April. The Government dropped it for want of time to carry both it and measures thought more important through their stages in the House. *The Times* greeted it with a lengthy lead editorial on 5 April 1890, favoring the bill in a tired, hopeless fashion: "No Session is complete without an Employers' Liability Bill. This hardy annual makes its reappearance in the Queen's Speech with the regularity of Spring." After a lengthy and scholarly discussion of the issues, *The Times* went on to wish the measure well but noted in conclusion that, "all concerned look far beyond Employers' Liability Bills and in wholly different directions for a material improvement of the lot of working men. Opinion has altered much since 1880, when the present statute became law. Its successor has tarried so long on the way that no one now is very anxious about its arrival." The author of this paragraph may have been overly optimistic about "all concerned" but events proved him correct in the long run: Chamberlain and the Conservatives did indeed look far beyond Employers' Liability Bills.

It is worth noting that when the Permanent Secretary of the Home Office (Sir Godfrey Lushington) prepared an interoffice Confidential Memorandum on the subject of employers' liability, he made extensive use of the above article in *The Times:* he directly transcribed phrases, expressions, and entire arguments from the clipping to his Memorandum. Asquith (Home Secretary in Gladstone's 1892 Government) in turn relied heavily upon the Memorandum to prepare his speech on the second reading of the Employers' Liability Bill of 1893. Specifically, *The Times,* Lush-

31. PRO, H.O. 45/9819/B8164/1.

ington, and Asquith contended that, if unjust or harsh, the common law on the subject of employers' liability at least was intelligible: it was logical to say that a servant had parted, for his wages, with the right of action which he would have had in respect of injuries caused by a fellow servant. Once abandon that principle and no middle course will suffice short of that advocated by Mr. Burt in 1891: the total abolition of the doctrine of common employment. Included, of course, was the prohibition of any contracting out, for the object of the legislation was to avoid anomalies by rendering the employer as answerable to his servants as he was to the general public. Any attempt to permit contracting out must include safeguards which guarantee that the workman does not enter into such a contract except for good consideration. In the event such consideration is deemed unsatisfactory (however that may be determined) the workman must be free to break his bargain and recover independently of his contract. The article in *The Times* took violent exception to this final conclusion: "Nothing which creates a peculiar class of persons, be they rich or poor, privileged to break their promises can be unobjectionable."

Whatever *The Times,* and later Asquith, may have said, the labor unions were as firm in their opposition to the 1890 Government bill as they had been to that of 1888. At the Annual Conference of the Miners' Federation of Great Britain, held in Nottingham on 11 April, a resolution was unanimously carried expressing "entire disapproval" of the bill and urging all members of Parliament representing mining constituencies to be in their places to support the labor members in opposing the bill at the second reading and subsequent stages. A month after the Government withdrew the bill, a resolution was unanimously passed at the Annual Meeting of Anthracite Miners and Other Workmen on 30 August 1890 urging that an "improved Employers' Liability Bill should be introduced next session." The improvements recommended were to prohibit contracting out of the Act altogether; to materially limit the doctrine of common employment; to make the principal contractor liable in all cases of subcontract; and to fix no limit to the damages recoverable.[32] On 10 January 1891 a similar resolution was unanimously carried at the Conference of the Miners' Confederation, a union which claimed to represent 212,000 workmen connected with the mining industry.

The Conservatives never again introduced another Employers' Liability Bill. That remained for the Liberals, who returned to office under Gladstone in 1892.

32. Ibid. pp. 1, 10.

CHAPTER 4

Personalities: Gladstone and Asquith

The late 1880s saw a period of growing industrial and social unrest in England. The agricultural depression, which began in 1879, reached its height in 1886 and was reflected in a general depression throughout the British Isles. The depression was so severe that a Royal Commission was appointed to inquire into its causes. It reported in 1887, not more enlightened than when it started. Discontent among the unemployed was reflected in a whole series of demonstrations. In February 1886 a small "army" organized by the Social Democratic Federation invaded a Fair Trade demonstration being conducted in Trafalgar Square. Having dispossessed the demonstrators of Trafalgar Square, the mob surged through the shopping centers of the West End, smashing windows, overturning carriages, and generally terrorizing the neighborhood. For over two hours they ran unchecked before the police were able to restore order. Another series of demonstrations broke out in the autumn of 1887. In November a serious conflict between mob and authority again occurred in Trafalgar Square. So menacing was the mob that the police enlisted the aid of a battalion of Foot Guards and two squadrons of the Life Guards to disperse them.[1]

It may be significant that the Oxford English Dictionary gives the first use of the word "unemployment" in 1888. Certainly the period under consideration saw a rapidly growing self-awareness in the laboring classes. It grew partly owing to the extended franchise, partly to the above demonstrations, but mostly to the trades disputes. Strikes occurred with growing frequency and (by then current standards) increasing severity: in 1888 alone there

1. Sir J. A. R. Marriott, *Modern England, 1885-1932* (London, Methuen, 1934), p. 36.

were over 500 strikes, and 1889 saw the famous London Dockers' Strike.

This last held great significance for the future of unionism in England: on the London docks the more skilled workers had already combined into a Stevedores' Union; the great mass of unskilled longshoremen were unorganized and their employment was entirely casual and intermittent. Under the leadership of a fiery orator named Ben Tillet they were persuaded to organize into a union and strike for a uniform rate of pay (sixpence an hour) for a minimum of four hours per day. The dock companies resisted their demands until it became clear that not only the shipowners but the general public as well were on the side of the strikers: subscriptions, amounting to nearly £50,000, poured in from sympathizers, and within a month the dockers got their "tanner."[2]

From this strike dates the New Unionism: membership in a union no longer would be exclusively composed of skilled workmen or artisans. In a very short time the number of men enrolled in unions took an enormous jump. A quite typical example is the Miners' Federation of Great Britain: from 36,000 members in 1888 it could claim to represent 212,000 miners in 1891. With this fantastic growth in numbers came a realization of the political strength of organized labor, out of which eventually grew the present day Labor party. According to R. C. K. Ensor, the leaders of the New Unionism were conscious socialists who intended, by means of parliamentary control, to effect fundamental changes in the structure of society. That story lies beyond this study; but already in the 1890s Parliament began to take the demands of the trade unions much more seriously than it had in the 1880s.

At the same time businessmen, and most particularly the shipping interests, found themselves confronted with the imposition of punitive protective tariffs abroad, aimed specifically at British exports. Coupled with the enormous growth of the industrial po-

2. Ibid., pp. 35–39.

tential of the European countries (mostly Germany) and the United States, the tariffs placed Britain in a disadvantageous position in the world markets. Faith in the principles of free trade lessened accordingly, and insofar as free trade was associated with the Manchester School, that school, with its belief in laissez-faire for domestic affairs, also suffered a loss of prestige.

Gladstone's convictions placed him squarely in the Manchester School, at least in relation to domestic policies. His preoccupation with the Irish question, amounting as it did to an obsession, belonged entirely to that school's concern with administrative and constitutional questions, and not at all to the more modern concern for economic and social problems. Throughout his life he had invariably appealed to broad abstract principles, with the object of making men worthier citizens by enhancing their capacities. Gladstone addressed his emotional appeal over the heads of the upper ten thousand directly to the moral and religious instincts of the masses, and it was this emotional oratory which accounted for his enormous popularity. In the great days of his feud with Disraeli it was this characteristic appeal to broad principles which most irritated the latter. Disraeli had no patience with the notion that all important political questions involved clear-cut moral issues; he considered that, in an imperfect world, the choice must lie between policies of varying degrees of expediency. Gladstone believed that men who thought like that were corrupted by the insolence of wealth and privilege. For all the moral deterioration and corruption which Gladstone thought had occurred in public life in his time he blamed only Disraeli, for he believed him to be wholly without principles or convictions of any kind.[3] He thrust on Disraeli the blame for the demoralization of Chamberlain and Churchill, whom he regarded with grave misgivings. In 1887 he remarked to Edward Hamilton,

> If I were in a dying condition, I confess I should have one great apprehension in my mind—what I conceive to be the

3. Magnus, *Gladstone: A Biography,* pp. 256, 381.

greatest danger to my country. It is not Ireland. That difficulty will be solved. It is not the character of future measures. The good sense of the people will take care of those. It is the men of the future—personalities of the stamp of Randolph Churchill and Chamberlain.[4]

As a member of the Manchester School, Gladstone entertained strong suspicions about the desirability of state interference in the lives of its citizens; but he clearly foresaw that such meddling must occur, not from any intrinsic necessity but because such was the intention of men like Chamberlain and Churchill. In a letter to Lord Acton dated 11 February 1885 he wrote, "There is no crisis at all in view. There is a process of slow modification and development, mainly in directions which I view with misgivings. . . . Its pet idea is what they call construction—that is to say taking into the hands of the State the business of the individual man."[5] In this idea of "construction" Gladstone found "much to estrange" him. "Collectivism," "construction," and "socialism" were favorite pejoratives with him, and he remained antipathetic to the ideas behind such words until his death. Gladstone proposed to meet the challenge of socialism by the voluntary distribution of wealth by the wealthy. In this he heartily endorsed the views expressed in Andrew Carnegie's book, *The Gospel of Wealth.* He urged that rich men should all follow the example of Carnegie by distributing a substantial portion of their wealth during their lifetimes. Gladstone followed this precept himself, every year giving away a large part of his own income.[6] With regard to "construction" (a mixture of state interference and social reform) his belief in laissez-faire never faltered: in 1891, for instance, he was asked by a gas worker about his views on the Eight-Hour Bill. He replied, "When I am asked to impose legal penalties upon any workman who desires and

4. Ibid., p. 370.
5. Garvin, *Joseph Chamberlain, 1,* 173.
6. Magnus, p. 258.

agrees to work more than eight hours per day . . . I must pause before agreeing to this affliction."[7]

It seems peculiar, therefore, that in 1891 the Liberal party, under his auspices, adopted a platform composed of thoroughly meddlesome planks. The leading article of the Newcastle Program (as it came to be called) was of course Home Rule for Ireland, followed by church disestablishment in Scotland and Wales, a local veto on the sale of intoxicating liquors, "one man, one vote" (abolition of the plural franchise), triennial Parliaments, and, for labor, an improved employers' liability law. The truth of the matter seems to have been that Gladstone became a little negligent in his old age about the means he employed to achieve his ends. Much of the Newcastle Program was extremely distasteful to him and he made no attempt to digest some parts of it at all.[8] The bulk of his party having deserted him over Home Rule, to which he was absolutely committed, Gladstone was pushed into radicalism against his will in order to win the 1892 election. It was, however, a radicalism of a different order from that of Chamberlain. It aimed at what came to be known as the Celtic Fringe (Scotland and Wales), hence the inclusion of local veto and church disestablishment in the Newcastle Program, both of which were dear to those two countries. Gladstone had had it gradually made clear to him that his Irish policy at best held a weakening appeal, and further that the demands of the new radicalism were going to have to be met by any party that wanted to get elected. So when the Liberal Caucus held a gigantic meeting at Newcastle-on-Tyne on 1 and 2 October 1891, it was with this object—election—in mind that they adopted a collection of secondhand radical ideas not unified by any internal consistency. Gladstone had not changed, and though he gave his blessing to the program in a speech at Newcastle on 2 October, no one took

7. William J. Wilkinson, *Tory Democracy* (New York, Columbia University Press, 1925), p. 171.
8. Magnus, p. 396.

him seriously. Gladstone had overcome his repugnance for the sake of Home Rule; his advocacy of the program represented a concession, not a conviction.

Gladstone was immensely disappointed by the election results, for instead of a majority in the hundreds, as he had expected, he was returned to office with a majority of forty. This should have been enough to persuade him that he had no clear mandate from the people for his Home Rule policy. In the event, it was only personal loyalty to him that induced his Cabinet to follow in his quixotic course, for any Home Rule bill clearly stood no chance of passing the House of Lords. There Lord Salisbury controlled an enormous Conservative majority, and Salisbury was committed on the basis of personal conviction to the maintenance of the integrity of the Empire. Nonetheless, Gladstone pursued his course, for at the age of 83 only his sense of an obligation to finally settle the Irish question in favor of Home Rule motivated him to remain in politics at all.

Accordingly he introduced his Second Home Rule Bill in the House of Commons in February 1893; the second reading passed on 21 April and the third reading on 1 September. When it finally passed the Commons, it had occupied that House's attention for 85 sittings and virtually the entire summer. Gladstone exhibited prodigious endurance in personally guiding the measure through all its stages. The House of Lords, after hearing a prolonged speech in opposition by Salisbury, rejected the measure on 8 September by 419 to 91. The defeat should have surprised no one, least of all Gladstone. But in his bitterness he attributed the Lords' behavior to purely partisan motives. Since, however, virtually the entire Whig peerage had deserted him in 1886 on precisely this issue, the charge of partisanship seems clearly unfounded.

Far and away the most brilliant member of Gladstone's Cabinet was Herbert Henry Asquith. A barrister of forty, who had been elected to Parliament in 1886, he became almost at once the most

brilliant Home Secretary within living memory. At the time the
post was offered to him he had never held even the most minor
governmental position.

Though Asquith spoke infrequently in Parliament (no more
than two or three times per year for his first six years) his speeches
had considerable impact. In his maiden speech he assumed at once
the authoritative tone of a front bencher whose opinions should be
listened to not for the weight of their argument, but for the weight
of the holder of those opinions; and the Commons accepted him
at his own valuation. Asquith remained a staunch supporter of
Gladstone. After Chamberlain and his Liberal Unionists left the
party, Asquith opposed making too many concessions to lure them
back. At a meeting of the National Liberal Federation at Nottingham (18 October 1887) he moved a resolution of confidence in the
policy of Home Rule: speaking, as he said, as a very humble member of the Liberal party, he thought the limits of concession to the
Unionists had been reached; Henry IV had thought Paris worth
a mass, but they might pay too high a price for the capitulation of
Birmingham. Asquith concluded his address with a tribute to
Gladstone,

> whose presence at our head is worth a hundred battalions.
> To the youngest it is an inspiration; to the oldest an example,
> to one and all a living lesson of devotion, hopefulness and
> vitality. . . . Let us, lesser men of a later day, be proud that
> in such an enterprise and under such omens we are permitted
> to obey his summons and follow when he leads.[9]

When the Commons finally got around to investigating charges
that one of its members, Parnell, had certainly sanctioned and
probably was implicated in the Irish Phoenix Park murders involving the death of Lord Cavendish, Asquith was named as-
sistant defense counsel for Parnell. After the chief defense counsel,
Sir Charles Russel, had demolished Richard Pigott, the forger of

9. Spender and Asquith, *Life of Herbert Henry Asquith, 1,* 57.

the letters which formed the basis for the charges against Parnell, the cross-examination of the manager of *The Times,* which had printed the letters, fell to Asquith. He conducted his examination brilliantly, ruthlessly, and with dispatch. Inside of two hours he had established that the manager, Macdonald, had accepted the letters as genuine on the basis of personal dislike for Parnell, having made no effort whatsoever to establish their veracity, and had behaved throughout the whole affair "with a credulity which would have been childlike if it had not been criminally negligent."[10]

To have played so material a part in unmasking the anti-Irish machinations of *The Times* and in vindicating Parnell would have constituted a real boost to the aspirations of any politician in Gladstone's Liberal party; for Asquith, already easily achieving recognition as a rising force in the depleted Liberal ranks, it meant a virtually assured position of power in the next Liberal Government. On 14 August 1892, overcoming his principle of using only men with considerable ministerial experience for top cabinet positions, Gladstone offered Asquith the post he coveted above all others. Asquith accepted with alacrity.

Though Gladstone's fourth Government was highly unsuccessful, Asquith proved an exceptionally fine Home Secretary, "the best of the century," writes Gladstone's most recent biographer.[11] By the end of his term in office, he was the one minister who could be depended upon never to make a bad speech. He got along well with Gladstone because he made his own decisions and did not disturb the Prime Minister's Irish brooding. Recognized as a moderate innovator, Asquith liked to move, but only in well-tried directions.[12]

As a young man Asquith took a first in classics at Balliol College, Oxford. The extraordinary success—both in politics and business—of Balliol men in the last quarter of the nineteenth century has often been remarked upon; Asquith is a prime example. Such

10. Roy Jenkins, *Asquith* (London, Collins, 1964), p. 49.
11. Magnus, p. 402.
12. Jenkins, p. 63.

success has largely been attributed to the influence of its Master, Benjamin Jowett, upon his students, for Jowett preached a gospel of work. Though a clergyman, Jowett strongly believed that want of worldly success is no necessary index of spiritual distinction. He recoiled violently from ideology and had no taste for abstract speculation; rather he was concerned with the workability of institutions, not with their abstract symmetry or perfection. He believed, nonetheless, that the best intellectuals of the nation should direct its destinies and had no use for fugitive or secluded thinkers who shrank from commitment to the affairs of the world.[13]

His gospel of work was entirely secular: work for work's sake with scarcely any attention paid to the ends aimed at. The means thus became ends in themselves. Jowett rarely mentioned religious or ethical principles, preferring to concern himself with pure technique. Thus a letter to Lord Lansdowne upon the latter's receipt of a Second at Balliol contains the following rather curious advice for a clergyman to forward to his charge: "[for the successful man] Time will show him how to shape his course. . . . Knowledge of the world and of political subjects; reticence, self-control, freedom from personal feeling, are the qualities to be aimed at."[14]

Jowett was Master of Balliol College while Asquith was an undergraduate. Thus the relationship of tutor to pupil never existed between the two. They had, however, considerable contact at breakfast, on long walks, and during the dreaded "mauvais quarts d'heures" of a Balliol undergraduate when he had to read his weekly essay aloud to the Master.[15] Whether Asquith acquired his addiction to hard work from Jowett, or merely had it reinforced; and whether he acquired his suspicion of abstract thinking from Jowett, or merely had it confirmed, are questions which will not be answered, for Asquith also shared Jowett's veneration of reticence. Not even his own children ever fathomed Asquith's

13. Spender and Asquith, *1*, 36.
14. Melvin Richter, *The Politics of Conscience: T. H. Green and His Age* (Cambridge, Harvard University Press, 1964), p. 66.
15. Spender and Asquith, *1*, 36.

religious and ethical thinking, though his son and first biographer, Cyril Asquith, has written that, at least in his suspicion "that obscurity of expression has its origin in muddy, not profound, thinking," Asquith was heavily influenced by Jowett. Clearly, therefore, Asquith should have been predisposed to regard the teachings of his tutor, T. H. Green, with some suspicion, for the latter, if nothing else, was obscure. But despite such suspicions, Asquith had the most profound respect and admiration for Green.[16]

Already when Asquith arrived at Balliol in 1869, T. H. Green was acknowledged to be the great man of the college. That Green influenced Asquith is beyond dispute, for the latter was a friend of Green, and attended his lectures as well as having him for a tutor. Furthermore, Asquith approved of Green's politics, for Green was an active and an ardent Liberal.[17] H. J. Laski, on the basis of personal conversations with Asquith, has remarked, "I know of no better illustration of the impact of [Green's] work than in its effect upon an eminent politician like the late Earl of Oxford, who, as Mr. Asquith, held office under Mr. Gladstone, and was himself Prime Minister."[18]

While Green is chiefly remembered for his political philosophy, his ethics provided the cornerstone of his thinking and must be considered, if cursorily, for that reason. He early discarded the atomistic position adopted by Hume, for inevitably that position's acceptance of strict causality led to a conclusion of no moral responsibility on the part of the individual for his personal conduct. Green preferred to regard man as characterized by a fully integrated personality which is conscious of change, not merely as a passive recipient of transitory sense perceptions. Green further believed (with the German Idealists) that the individual, through the exercise of will, could alter the course of events in an

16. Ibid., p. 37.
17. Jenkins, p. 23.
18. Harman Grisewood, ed., *Ideas and Beliefs of the Victorians* (London, Sylvan Press, 1949), p. 420.

otherwise causally determined world. Since the exercise of that will directly influenced other persons, the highest duty of any such agent must be to insure that the will was appropriately guided, both in himself and in others. Accordingly self-development and the development of individual character were the principal goals to be sought after. The duty of the state (since duty did exist and since Green accepted the state as an active moral agent) was to maintain those rights and obligations necessary to the development of individual character.[19]

Green agreed with Bentham and Mill in objecting to any talk about "natural rights" and would have grounded the state's duty on social expediency. But while Mill would ultimately have brought "social expediency" around to a consideration of pleasures and pains, Green insisted that social expediency was ultimately determined by the scope which any measure gave to the individual for exercising all his capacities of self-development. And all true self-development involved considerations of the well-being of the community.[20]

Although the contrary is generally alleged, Green most emphatically was not the philosopher of collectivism. He found his model man of politics, both in conduct and belief, in the person of John Bright.[21] Green believed that every proposed state action must be measured and weighed in terms of its effect on individual character, and he frequently asserted that the sole acceptable province for state activity lay in hindering hindrances to the good life. In this he was at once echoing Kant and generalizing from the principles used by the Manchester School to destroy monopolies said to be blocking the natural development of individual initiative. Kant states in his "Philosophy of Law" that

> if a certain exercise of freedom is itself a hindrance of the Freedom that is [growth] according to Universal Laws, it is

19. "Thomas Hill Green," *Encyclopedia Britannica*, 11th ed. *12*, 535.

20. David G. Ritchie, *The Principles of State Interference* (London, Swan Sonnenschein, 1891), p. 144.

21. Richter, p. 77.

wrong; and the compulsion or constraint which is opposed
to it is right, as being a hindering of a hindrance of Freedom,
and as being in accord with the Freedom which exists in accordance with Universal Laws.[22]

Green took violent exception to what he conceived to be the principle of paternal government:

> The true ground of objection to "paternal government" is
> not that it violates the laissez-faire principle and conceives
> that its office is to make people good, to promote morality,
> but that it rests on a misconception of morality. The real
> function of government being to maintain conditions of life
> in which morality shall be possible, and morality consisting
> in the disinterested performance of self-imposed duties,
> "paternal government" does its best to make it impossible by
> narrowing the room for the self-imposition of duties and for
> the play of disinterested motives.[23]

Despite these objections, Green was obliged by his very insistence upon self-realization to accept a limited position in favor
of what Sir Isaiah Berlin has called "positive freedom." He was
obliged to maintain that true freedom involves more than a man's
mere ability to do as he prefers to do in a given instance, irrespective of what it is that he prefers to do. Rather true freedom means
"the greater power on the part of the citizens as a body to make the
most and best of themselves."[24] Berlin has denounced in stinging
terms the central idea which lies behind all theories of government
involving self-realization and a "positive" notion of freedom:
"This monstrous impersonation which consists in equating what
X would choose if he were something he is not, or at least not yet,
with what X actually seeks and chooses, is at the heart of all politi-

22. Ibid., p. 271.
23. Ibid., p. 236.
24. Ibid., p. 204.

cal theories of self-realization."[25] Green seems to have sensed the danger in his position, for he drew back from and resisted the ultimate conclusion that the whole is superior to the part, the state to the individual. Green had grave misgivings about redefining freedom to mean, not absence of constraint, but the power to realize only those capacities involved in man's *telos*. Accordingly he ringed his injunctions with safeguards, determined to prevent an abuse of his permission to employ collective action. Specifically, he insisted that collective action was to be judged solely by its effect upon the individual, not the community:

> There can be nothing in a nation, however exalted its mission, or in a society, however perfectly organized, which is not in the persons composing the nation or the society. Our ultimate standard of worth is an ideal of *personal* worth. All other values are relative to value for, of, or in a person. To speak of any progress or improvement or development of a nation or society or mankind, except as relative to some greater worth of persons, is to use words without meaning.[26]

Precisely because of the dichotomy in his thinking between positive freedom and strong safeguards against its abuse, his followers have been able to take entirely divergent positions on the question of state interference: either against it on the basis of its adverse effects upon self-reliance and personal character, or in favor of it because of the obligations of the community to its members.[27] Nonetheless, Green's "freedom *to* develop" theories seem to have liberated many Liberals from the narrow individualism of the Manchester School, which held that freedom consisted entirely in being free *from* any sort of restraint. On the question of compulsory education, for example, the possibility was pointed out that an increase in governmental activity might add to the liberty of

25. Isaiah Berlin, *Two Concepts of Liberty* (Oxford, Clarendon Press, 1958), p. 18.
26. Richter, p. 209.
27. Ibid., p. 212.

individuals rather than diminish it: "It is not as a purely moral duty on the part of a parent, but as the prevention of a hindrance to the capacity for rights on the part of children, that education should be enforced [made compulsory] by the State."[28] Furthermore, his emphasis on true citizenship amounted almost to a religion, for he "reckoned it higher than saintliness"; his attempts to arouse a sense of guilt in the upper classes seem to have met with a certain measure of success: in the seventies and eighties he was hailed as the spokesman for the new movement of the evangelical impulse. Beatrice Webb writes in *My Apprenticeship:*

> The origin of the ferment is to be discovered in a new consciousness of sin . . . , a collective or class consciousness; a growing uneasiness, amounting to conviction, that the industrial organization, which had yielded rent, interest and profits on a stupendous scale, had failed to provide a decent livelihood and tolerable conditions for a majority of the inhabitants of Great Britain.[29]

After Green's death in 1882, his numerous disciples generally went their separate ways, each taking that part of the master's thought which suited him best. Arnold Toynbee adapted his teaching to the needs of the Radical wing of the Liberal party. In an address given in London in 1883 entitled "Are Radicals Socialists?" Toynbee stated in part:

> The radical creed is this: We have not abandoned our old belief in liberty, justice, and self-help, but we say that under certain conditions the people cannot help themselves, and that then they should be helped by the State representing directly the whole people. In giving this State help we make three conditions: first, the matter must be one of primary social importance; next, it must be proved to be practicable; thirdly, the State interference must not diminish self-reliance.

28. Ritchie, p. 148.
29. Richter, p. 135.

Even if the chance should arise of removing a great social evil,
nothing must be done to weaken those habits of self-reliance
and voluntary association which have built up the greatness
of the English people.

Toynbee went on in the speech to draw a distinction between his
position and that of the Tory radicals, claiming that the Tories
advocated "paternal" government whereas his wing advocated
"fraternal" government.[30]

Bernard Bosanquet followed Green very closely in his book
entitled *The Philosophical Theory of the State,* but the first edition
of that work was not published until 1899 and accordingly has no
bearing on this study. In 1891, however, David G. Ritchie published *The Principles of State Interference,* a collection of four
essays on nineteenth-century political thinkers, including one on
T. H. Green which had first appeared in the *Contemporary Review*
in June 1887. The article, basically a polemic against state interference except under certain rigidly defined circumstances, made
much of one of Green's conclusions, namely, that a politician is not
wrong for opposing all such state action as tends to strengthen
some at the cost of others' weakness.

While we cannot assert that Asquith was in contact with and
influenced by the followers of T. H. Green, like Toynbee, Bosanquet, or Ritchie, it seems reasonable to assume that Green at
least influenced him in the same direction as these other thinkers.
Asquith had been tutored by Green; prominent young members
of his own party acknowledged Green as their mentor; in the last
twenty years of the nineteenth century, Green's thought received
a great deal of attention in the Liberal-oriented news media; and
Laski, who knew Asquith, believed him to have been greatly
influenced by Green. On the face of it the influence cannot be
doubted. In addition, Asquith's own behavior during the struggle
over the Employers' Liability Bill of 1893 supports the contention.

30. Ibid., p. 289.

CHAPTER 5

Employers' Liability Bill of 1893

In 1892 both political parties had committed themselves to some modification of the law relating to employers' liability: the Conservatives had announced their commitment by twice introducing an Employers' Liability Bill during their own administration; the Liberals had pledged themselves to a reform in the Newcastle Program. Chamberlain was, in a very real sense, the inheritor of Lord Randolph Churchill's post as the leader of the radical wing of the Conservative party. He had not yet formally changed allegiance, but had found that his policies met with a surprisingly favorable response from the Tories. Most important, he and Salisbury had overcome their mutual antipathy and could work together. In the Liberal party Gladstone had, if not overcome, at least been able to ignore, his objections to the Newcastle Program for the sake of Home Rule. Asquith, as we shall see, had been sufficiently exposed to the thought of T. H. Green to countenance governmental interference for the sake of "hindering hindrances to freedom." It was clear that some sort of Employers' Liability Bill would be introduced and passed.

Gladstone kissed hands for the fourth time on 15 August 1892 and immediately immersed himself and the bulk of his Government in preparing their Second Home Rule Bill. Asquith was not included in this select group, the responsibility for preparing the Government's promised Employer's Liability Bill having devolved to him instead. This task he had completed by 2 February 1893, and the bill he introduced to the House of Commons on that date bore his name and the names of the Attorney-General, Herbert Gladstone, and our old friend, E. A. Burt. The first version of the 1893 Employers' Liability Bill (No. 118), while refreshingly simple, contained several curious clauses. Of those more will be said later. In its opening clause it sought to abolish the defense of common employment by declaring that henceforth, when personal injury was caused to a workman by reason of the negligence of any person in the service of the workman's employer, the workman (or his representative) "shall have the same right to compensation and remedies against the employer as if the workman had not been a workman of, nor in the service of, the employer."[1] While such language may sound unnecessarily obscure, it makes abundantly clear Asquith's desire not to grant preferential treatment to one segment of the people over another; at the same time it sought to end the worker's complaint that his contract of service was being used as an instrument of exploitation, or at least discrimination, against him by the courts.

As did the 1880 Act, Asquith's bill contained a clause stating in effect that where a workman knew of the negligence which caused his accident, and failed within a reasonable time to give notice thereof to either his employer or someone in authority, he would have no right of action under the Act. Asquith softened this injunction by adding that such failure must be without "reasonable excuse." Nonetheless, such language effectively preserved the defense of *Volenti non fit injuria:* knowing of the deficiency, a workman was to be barred from recovery unless he evidenced some disinclination to remain at work under such circumstances. Naturally, contracting out was forbidden: any contract whereby the worker relinquished his rights under the Act would not bar recovery in court.

In the event the employer contributed to the worker's Friendly Society, and the injured worker elected to sue the employer instead of claiming against the fund, Clause 3 of the bill entitled the employer to any money which would have been payable out of the fund to the worker. Clause 4 declared that any fine paid to the worker by the employer in pursuance of any Act of Parliament (e.g.

1. PRO, H.O. 45/9865/B13816/1.

under one of the Factory Acts) would be deducted from any compensation awarded as a result of a suit under the Act. By these two curious provisions Asquith clearly intended to mitigate any tendencies of the Act to induce employers to withdraw their support of the Friendly Societies, and at the same time to insure that the employer did not pay twice for the same offense.

The Government wasted no time in bringing its Employers' Liability Bill to the attention of the Commons. The second reading was scheduled for 20 February, and as approval of the second reading constitutes approval of the principle of the bill, it is with the debate on the second reading that we are concerned.

Asquith arose, "amid cheers," to move the second reading, and prefaced his discussion of the provisions of the bill with a brief history of employers' liability. He emphasized that so long as industry had remained on a small scale with employer and workman in close contact, the employer's liability for his own negligence was an adequate source of relief for the injured workman; but with the growth of large scale industries organized into corporations it had become increasingly difficult for the injured workman to bring home to the person from whom he received his wages personal knowledge and responsibility for the loss which he had sustained. While, as we have seen, this analysis does not correspond exactly to the facts (legal remedies had never been anywhere close to adequate), it nonetheless took into account the debilitating effects of modern, impersonal industry on the workman's morale.

Asquith argued that, unable to bring home to the master his responsibility on the basis of personal negligence, the workman was obliged to invoke "another principle of our law—the principle that a master or principal is responsible for the acts of his agent or servant in the course and within the scope of their duty," in short the rule of vicarious liability. But, he alleged, when the courts came to decide that question, they elected on the ground of policy to treat the servant as an exception to the general rule; "they invented an implied contract on the part of the workman to take upon

himself . . . the negligence of his fellow-servant." Calling common
employment a "fictitious doctrine" to which the laboring classes
had never assented, Asquith listed for an increasingly emotional
House the "manifold and overwhelming" objection to it: no such
contract is ever entered into, and in any event the common law
goes upon the sound and sensible principle that when two parties
enter into an agreement they must be taken to have meant what
they say; the doctrine places the workman in a worse position than
any stranger, for "if a train is run off the line through the ignorance,
inattention, or want of skill of the engine-driver," the passengers
may recover damages but not the stoker and the guard; the rule,
furthermore, works unequally as between small employers and
large since the latter dispose of their liability by delegating authority; lastly, common employment operates as a distinct tempta-
tion to the employer to neglect safety precautions, for without
liability there exists no inducement for the employer to exercise
that degree of care which his duty to his servants requires.[2]

Asquith mentioned the history of legislation on the subject and
then identified his Government with the labor representatives
(Burt and Broadhurst) and the principle behind their employers'
liability bills introduced year after year in the 1880s, namely the
total abolition of the doctrine of common employment and the
prohibition of contracting out. He justified this abolition by in-
voking two principles which, considering the moralizing tendencies of the age, were surprisingly modern. One was vicarious
liability: "We think that the general rule of law that a master
ought to be liable for the acts or omissions of his servants is a good
rule, and that it is a rule which might be applied on the same
grounds of justice and expediency in the case of a workman as in
the case of a stranger." The other was the ground of strict liability:
"Where a person on his own responsibility sets in motion agencies
which create risk for others, he ought to be civilly responsible for
the consequences."

2. PRO, H.O. 45/9865/B13816/13.

Although both of these principles could be found in the common law at that time, both were ultimately grounded in policy: someone who is able to pay should have to pay. Of course, any action under the proposed bill had ultimately to be grounded in the negligence of someone in the master's employ; but the master himself was to pay for that negligence, and the element of his *culpa* was missing.

Having invoked the two principles above, neither one making any appeal to the ethical sense of right and wrong, Asquith proceeded to discuss the limitations that the law would impose on an employer's liability:

> It will undoubtedly be open to an employer . . . to raise the defense of contributory negligence—that the workman, by his own act or omission, is a contributory cause to the injury he sustained. If without that act or omission either the accident would not have occurred or would not have been attended with the injurious consequences which followed it, then it would not be *fair,* and the law would not allow, that the master should be held liable.[3]

It is around precisely this issue that controversy raged, for after Asquith concluded his remarks, Joseph Chamberlain rose to move the following amendment:

> That no amendment of the law relating to employers' liability will be final or satisfactory which does not provide compensation to workmen for all injuries sustained in the ordinary course of their employment, and not caused by their own acts or default.[4]

Then, taking the floor, he attacked the Government bill on the ground that it did not settle "on lines broad and simple a long-standing controversy," and that it did not "place the law on a logical footing" (Asquith's introductory words). Chamberlain

3. Ibid.; emphasis supplied.
4. Ibid.

argued that under the present state of the law the employer's legal liability was equivalent to his moral liability: that when a man was injured either directly or indirectly through the employer's own personal misconduct or neglect, then the employer was penalized by the law. But the proposed legislation would go far beyond that and make the employer legally liable in cases where no one can say that he has any moral liability: "He is to be legally liable in pocket for matters over which he cannot possibly exercise any direct control." Giving as an example the case of a mining operation, Chamberlain sketched a situation where, under present law, the master would be liable: a disaster occurs owing to defects in ventilation of which the master should have been aware and for which he will be held liable. But under the proposed law the master will be held liable for a disaster caused by the stupidity or misconduct of one of his workmen.

> You have entered on a new principle. You are no longer punishing an employer for a matter in which he is morally liable, but you are fining him in order to provide compensation in the case of deaths or injury of people where he has had no moral liability whatever. . . . If you adopt the principle of this Bill you give up the idea of moral responsibility and you take the ground of expediency. You say that when a man is injured it is right that he should have compensation, and you are making the employer the channel of compensation.[5]

This basis, expediency, constituted the entire ground of Chamberlain's amendment. He went on to argue that, since the Government had accepted that position as well, they ought to be willing to carry it to its ultimate conclusion. This the bill clearly did not do, since, according to the best statistics available, well over half of the industrial accidents in the nation would be unaccounted for: they arose through no determinable negligence on anyone's part but through what the law called "acts of God." Chamberlain main-

5. Ibid.

tained that it was "the moral obligation of the House to provide that in every such case these persons [injured under circumstances not provided for by the bill] should be compensated as far as pecuniary compensation can be afforded." At the same time he wished to extend and render more stringent those provisions of the law which, by heavily penalizing the employer whenever his conduct was at fault, tended to make him properly careful in the conduct of his business.

Chamberlain's amendment and his argument in support of it were devastating. Asquith had had prior notice of the proposed amendment and attempted to answer it in his own speech before Chamberlain took the floor. He accused Chamberlain of trying to sabotage the Government bill by introducing an altogether new principle which would prevent the second reading being passed. The new principle Asquith thought Chamberlain had in mind was industrial insurance:

> Therefore the amendment comes to this: my right hon. friend is asking the House to reject this Bill—that is to say, to postpone giving to the workmen of this country two amendments of the law upon which they are all united, and in support of which they have behind them a vast and preponderating body of public opinion, for a period of possibly five or ten years, until some one has ingenuity enough to devise such a system of insurance.[6]

And Asquith objected to industrial insurance on the ground that it affords no security or incentive for the exercise of care on the part of the employer. Also he objected that "it involves an amount of official interference upon the part of the State which I do not think either the employers or workmen of this country would tolerate." The choice seemed to Asquith to be between adopting a remedy which, being "practicable," could come into operation at once, or "expressing . . . an academic opinion in favor of a general

6. Ibid.

system of industrial insurance, which nobody is prepared to put down upon the paper, and which cannot come into operation for years to come."

These arguments sum up, by implication, Asquith's intellectual baggage: like Toynbee,[7] he would undertake that the state should help the people if the matter was of primary and proven importance and if the people as a whole were behind it: but the means "must be proved to be practicable" and must not involve so large a degree of state interference as to alter habits of self-reliance. With Jowett, he entertained strong suspicions of abstract academic thinking, preferring to concern himself with the workability of institutions.[8] As a Liberal strongly influenced by both Gladstone and T. H. Green, he was highly suspicious of anything which resembled either "construction" or "paternal government"; and as a lawyer he insisted on grounding his legislative proposals on principles, if not well-established, at least present in the common law.

In any case the Trades Union Congress came to his assistance, albeit in the most backhanded fashion imaginable. Evidence of this appears in the debate of 24 March, still on the second reading. During the course of his speech Mr. Bousfield remarked that he was sorry to see that certain labor and trade union representatives in the House had held a meeting in which they adopted a resolution of a curious character, to the effect that, as the Trades Union Congress had not demanded that all accidents should be met by insurance, they could not approve of Chamberlain's amendment. He went on to remark that he was sorry to see that the more modern tendency of trade unionism was to support arrangements which kept employers and workmen at arms length, rather than to support those, like Mr. Chamberlain's, which brought them together amicably.[9] This view of the role of trade union activity seems to have been common at the time; as we shall see, it was based on the publicly avowed intentions of the trade union leaders

7. Anothe. of Green's pupils, see supra p. 55.
8. See supra p. 50.
9. Parliamentary Debates, Fourth Series, *10*, 1058.

themselves, and the antipathy to these views accounts for the eventual stalemate and failure of the bill.

On 25 April Chamberlain withdrew his amendment, stating that it had served his purpose of bringing before the attention of the House an alternative solution to the problem. He admitted to being pleased with the favorable response it had received from Members on both sides, but since it traversed the principle of the present bill, which he hoped would be passed into law with amendments, he was obliged to refrain from pressing it to a division. He then drew the battle lines for the debate to follow: controversy would center about the question of contracting out. The present bill, by excluding mutual arrangements of proven worth, failed to take care of well over half the industrial accidents in the nation; such mutual arrangements are entered into by employers to avoid litigation—not liability, since their contributions amount to more than their enforceable obligations could possibly total. Why, he inquired, when litigation is assured under the present bill, should the employers continue to support the Friendly Societies?[10]

With Chamberlain's amendment out of the way the second reading passed the House without a division.

During the course of his speech moving the second reading, Asquith had considered the question of contracting out as well as the doctrine of common employment. On this question the bill eventually foundered, and it is curious that the debate on the subject at this stage should have been so cursory and seemingly illogical. Asquith, a brilliant debater, floundered about for nearly half an hour endeavoring to justify the bill's prohibition of contracting out. He began with a history of the issue and mentioned the late (Conservative) Government's proposals, first that any question arising as to the adequacy of consideration for such a contract be finally determined by the Board of Trade or one of the Principal Secretaries (Bill of 1888); then the Conservative

10. Parliamentary Debates, Fourth Series, *11*, 1210.

Bill of 1890 in which the issue was to be decided in court during the course of a suit for compensation. Asquith overruled these proposals on the entirely specious ground that neither a department of the Government nor the courts had the requisite knowledge to give a satisfactory judgment as to whether such a contract was reasonable. He then produced the most vague and thoroughly contradictory evidence as to the extent of contracting out, the size of employers' contributions to Friendly Societies, and the attitude of the workmen themselves toward the issue. He concluded his discussion of the practical side of the question by announcing that "The conclusion to which the Government have come in view of these facts of the general considerations of policy affecting the case is that, for the future, a general prospective agreement by which a workman contracts himself out of the Act ought to be prohibited."[11]

In support of this position Asquith adduced the argument from the inequality of bargaining power, and stated that in some cases workmen were not altogether free agents and therefore could be coerced into accepting a contract which under different circumstances they would have shunned. While this position is sound, his further arguments are almost too embarrassingly illogical to report. Stating that, although in the case where Parliament conferred upon an individual or class a particular pecuniary benefit in their own interest alone they should have the right to abandon that benefit, such, he maintained, was not the present case: Here Parliament was interfering on the ground of "public policy and public safety"; the interference by the state was not in the interest of a particular class but was "in the interest of the community at large," and it should be out of the power of an individual to destroy by a private contract that safeguard imposed by Parliament. This was palpable nonsense.

At least part of the truth of the matter seems to have been that, with no limits placed on damages and with common employment

11. PRO, H.O. 45/9865/B13816/13.

abolished, the attractions of an occasional pound outweighed those of a certain penny in the minds of the representatives of organized labor; and it was to these bodies, the representatives of the New Unionism, that the Liberals were beholden for the slim majority they held in the House. On 24 March 1893 Mr. Woods, M.P., an official in the Miner's Federation of Great Britain, rose angrily to his feet and announced that he knew "absolutely so far as half a million of miners and a very large number of railway servants were concerned, that they wanted neither insurance nor contracting out on any condition whatever."[12] Although the amount recoverable was never mentioned as an argument, it was implied by the fanatical insistence of those opposed to contracting out that to permit the practice would free the employer from any inducement to exercise care. Those in favor of contracting out pointed out in vain that accidents caused by anyone's negligence—employer's or worker's—did not amount to even 40 per cent of the total of all industrial accidents. The opponents of contracting out were similarly unmoved by clear evidence that no discernible difference in the frequency of accidents existed between companies which had and companies which had not contracted their workers out of the existing law.

Whatever the reasons for the opposition by the unions to contracting out, the pressure they brought to bear on Asquith at the Home Office and the Government in general was heavy enough to preclude any compromise on the issue. From the time the bill was introduced until 15 December 1893 the Home Office received no less than 172 separate resolutions from various associations of workmen. Of these, 161 categorically opposed contracting out in any form (see Appendix II for a breakdown).[13] Throughout the entire debate on the bill, Asquith steadfastly resisted all attempts to remove or modify the clause prohibiting contracting out; when the bill was passed by the House of Commons with the clause still intact, its opponents shifted their attack to the House of Lords and

12. Ibid.
13. PRO, H.O. 45/9865/B13816.

there, as would be expected, met with success, for Conservatives were committed to contracting out by the previous Government.

But prior to that final stage the arguments had been thoroughly marshaled on boh sides. The trade union representatives steadfastly maintained that they were not concerned with compensation: what they wanted was protection from accidents in the first place. In order to get it they were entirely willing to see the employers withdraw their contributions to the Friendly Societies rather than have such contributions "shackle the free right of the workman to enforce his statutory remedy."[14]

The whole issue was immensely complicated by the case of the London and North Western Railway Company (L&NWRR). Throughout the entire debate both sides drew heavily on the available evidence, and both produced statements by workers in the company to support their positions.

Contracting out of the provisions of the 1880 Act and membership in a Friendly Society was a precondition of service on the L&NWRR. In consideration for such contract the railroad's management contributed on an exceptionally liberal scale to the insurance funds: their contribution amounted to slightly more than five-sixths of that of the employees. Injured workmen accordingly received remuneration on a generous scale. Annually the company contributed £8,000 to a Mutual Benefit Society, upward of £17,00 to the Mutual Insurance Fund (to which most of the employees belonged), and upward of £7,000 to the Locomotive Insurance Fund (to which the rest belonged). The authorities of the company unequivocally stated that in the event the Employers' Liability Bill was passed with the contracting out clause intact they would withdraw their contributions to the latter two funds.[15]

Asquith himself started the controversy in his speech moving the second reading of the bill. While dealing with the question of contracting out he mentioned that the general feeling among the 50,000 or so men employed by the L&NWRR ran counter to com-

14. PRO, H.O. 45/9865/B13816/33.
15. PRO, H.O. 45/9866/B13816/127.

pulsory contracting out irrespective of the generous contribution made by the company to the insurance funds. The following day Asquith received a lengthy letter from Mr. H. T. Cobb, a fellow Liberal in Parliament and colleague at Lincoln's Inn, who was in the employ of the L&NWRR. Cobb denied the truth of Asquith's statement the preceding day, declared that the men of the L&NWRR were so upset that they wished to send a deputation to set before Asquith their true views on the matter, which they considered to be of vital importance, and wondered if the afternoon of Saturday, 4 March, would be convenient for that purpose. Cobb emphasized that the deputation would consist of "representative" men in the Company's employ, none of whom would hold any official position which would in any way "limit or control absolute freedom and openness in speaking to you." He went on to say that as a result of personal inquiries he was convinced that the men were not only thoroughly in favor of the existing system, but also that they would regard any interference with it as a grave misfortune.

Asquith replied the following day agreeing to receive the deputation on 4 March. On 28 February he received an unsigned note postmarked from the Euston Station on the L&NWRR which read,

> Sir
>
> I wish to inform you that a deputation is about to wait upon you in reference to [the Employers' Liability Bill] composed chiefly of guards, Foremen and Underforemen, *not popularly* elected by the men.

In due course the deputation arrived and spoke out against the contracting out clause. Its views were publicized, although not in detail for much was made of the fact that no reporters (stenographers), who might have made the men "uneasy" were present to record their speeches verbatim.[16] When the debate on the second reading resumed on 24 March (it had been adjourned on

16. All based on PRO, H.O. 45/9865/B13816/24.

20 February), Mr. Woods attacked the credentials of the deputation saying that there were a number of railway contractors in the
House very much opposed to the Employers' Liability Bill, and he
respectfully submitted that it was a bogus deputation which did
not represent the railway servants of the country. He had personally addressed "hundreds of meetings of railway servants," and
had never met a single workman who was in favor of contracting
out. Challenged on this by another member, Woods announced
that that very morning he had received a letter from the secretary
of the Wigan branch of the L&NWRR saying that the deputation in
question did not represent the railway men on the subject.[17] (The
"secretary" who wrote the letter was the secretary of the local
branch of the Amalgamated Society of Railway Servants.)

Asquith was not impressed by the deputation and showed no
sign of altering his position. Labor rejoiced, and management re-
doubled its efforts: as the bill approached the stage when it went
before the Grand Committee on Law his desk was flooded with
personal letters from friends and business acquaintances urging
that he was injuring the interests of the workmen by refusing to
countenance equitable contracts, that his stubborn position would
lead to immense litigation and disrupt the amicable relations which
now existed between employer and employed, etc. Management of
the L&NWRR sent him letters postmarked from their various branch
offices urging that he please consider the wishes of their employees.
Asquith replied to these persons that his prohibition of contracting
out did not preclude the continued existence of Friendly Societies,
for after all there was evidence that they came into existence and
were supported by employers prior to 1880—before the practice
of contracting out came into being. The fallacies in his argument
are too obvious to require pointing out.

During May and June the Grand Committee on Law met six
times to discuss and amend the provisions of Asquith's bill. During
the third of these meetings, held on 1 June, the question of con-

17. PRO, H.O. 45/9865/B13816/11a.

tracting out arose; a Liberal member (Mr. Maclaren) moved that
it be permitted under certain circumstances, and argued from the
case of the L&NWRR that such an amendment would be in accordance with the expressed desires of the workers. Asquith rejected the proposal, argued at length that such was not the desire
of the majority of workers, that there was no reason why management of the L&NWRR should be granted special legislation, that the
bill in no way precluded continued contributions by employers to
Friendly Societies, and that in any case the object of the Bill was
to place the law on a sound and simple basis—not to create a mass
of litigious anomalies. The committee voted to reject Maclaren's
amendment[18] and the bill emerged from the committee with its
contracting-out clause intact in legal meaning, if obfuscated by
the addition of unnecessary words. The following day Asquith
received a letter from the Chief Inspector on the Joint Goods Staff
of the L&NWRR at Leeds, protesting the "injustice" of the action
taken by the committee and including a newspaper clipping from
the *Leeds Mercury* which recorded the enthusiasm felt by the
employees of the L&NWRR for their system of insurance.[19]

On 22 June the Grand Committee wound up its sixth and final
meeting on the bill, tabled its report before the House, and ordered
that the bill (now number 397) be printed "As amended before
the Grand Committee on Law" for the consideration of the House.
The committee had extended the benefits of the bill to include
employees of the Government, seamen, and domestic servants. The
story behind the inclusion of each of these, while dramatic and
enlightening as to the way the Government responded to pressure
groups, does not directly concern the eventual failure of the bill
except in the case of seamen; the inclusion of this group insured
the opposition of the powerful shipping interest lobby, a lesson
which would not be forgotten by Joseph Chamberlain when it
came his turn to guide the Workmen's Compensation Bill through
the House in 1897. The bill did not again come before the House

18. PRO, H.O. 45/9865/B13816/124.
19. PRO, H.O. 45/9865/B13816/120.

for formal consideration until its report stage, which began on 8 November. During the interim the House's attention was occupied with Gladstone and his Home Rule Bill; that story likewise lies beyond the scope of this book, although the heat engendered by the debate probably contributed in some measure to a partisan attitude toward the Employers' Liability Bill. Suffice it to say by way of illustration that tempers flared so strongly over the Home Rule Bill that on 27 July spectators in the House of Commons witnessed a riot scene during which several Members so forgot the rules of decorum as to punch one another in the nose. The incendiary word "Judas," hurled by an Irish Member at Chamberlain during the course of one of the latter's speeches in opposition to the bill, precipitated the riot, and only the dreaded rebuke of hissing from the gallery brought the House to its senses.[20]

Despite the excitement over Home Rule and Gladstone's famous marathon performance, the Employer's Liability Bill was not forgotten: on 29 June Mr. William Johnson wondered whether Asquith had seen a statement circulated by the Executive Committee appointed to watch the interests of the London and North Western Railway Insurance Society alleging that the bill would have a prejudicial effect on their position, and whether he would favorably consider any proposition allowing members of that and similar insurance societies to contract themselves out of the Act. Asquith replied that it was his considered opinion that the bill would not have the effect imagined by the circular, and that in any event the Grand Committee had decided "by a large majority to prevent contracting out of the Act," and to that decision the Government intended to adhere.[21] This rather ingenuous argument fooled no one, for, although the Grand Committee had been chaired by Matthew White Ridley (the future Home Secretary in Salisbury's third Government), its meeting times had conflicted with the scheduled meetings of the committee considering Gladstone's Home Rule Bill, and attendance by Opposition Members

20. Garvin, *The Life of Joseph Chamberlain,* 2, 573.
21. PRO, H.O. 45/9866/B13816/126.

had been minimal. In fact the decision to abide by the clause prohibiting contracting out had been Asquith's.

A new Member, Mr. Newdigate, pursued the point rather clumsily the following day. After a series of questions designed to point out the generous nature of the system of contracting out in the L&NWRR, he asked whether the Home Secretary had seen a circular letter issued from the London and North Western Railway Insurance Society, Members' Executive Office, Euston Station, in which it was alleged "that wrong impressions were conveyed throughout the debate in Committee" on the Employers' Liability Bill when the question of the attitude of the workers toward contracting out had been raised. Herbert Gladstone (the Prime Minister's son and Under Secretary of State for Home Affairs), speaking in Asquith's absence, replied that he had no such information and had not seen the circular. Mr. Newdigate then wondered whether the Home Secretary would consider the advisability of complying with the desire of the employees of the L&NWRR to be allowed to contract out of the Bill, and young Gladstone terminated the discussion by firmly announcing that Asquith had nothing to add to the answers given by him the day before to Mr. Johnson.[22]

From the introduction of the bill, contracting out slowly became the dominant subject of debate. Asquith's office was inundated weekly with dozens of letters: from management, all protesting the loss of a system so obviously beneficial to both sides; from labor unions, all commending him for his resolute stand on the clause. In addition, the Trades Union Congress unanimously passed a resolution calling for the Government to stand by its clause; their resolution was brought to the attention of the House on 7 September by means of a Government-planted question from the floor.[23] Petitioners on both sides of the argument sent him newspaper clippings giving reports of workmen who supported

22. PRO, H.O. 45/9866/B13816/127.
23. Parliamentary Debates, Fourth Series, 17, 466; PRO, H.O. 45/9866/B13816/181.

the petitioners' respective positions. Clearly, therefore, management was in favor of contracting out, labor union leaders opposed it, and the workers were of two minds on the subject. Later, in the report stage debates, this breakdown became increasingly apparent. By that time it had become obvious to all concerned that Asquith and the Government would not be budged, and contentious correspondence on the subject of contracting out disappeared from Asquith's Home Office mail altogether. The fight had not ended; it had shifted to other quarters.

Consideration of the Employers' Liability Bill began on the night of 8 November. Henry Matthews (Asquith's predecessor in the Home Office) passed along a few factious comments about the sloppy handling of the bill thus far and the paucity of uninterrupted debate, implying that had the Government not been so sneaky with its handling of the Committee stage, the bill would not now be in its present state of addled disrepair.[24] His speech prompted a general chorus of comments on the same subject, but eventually the bickering subsided and the House settled down to serious consideration of the bill. Immediately Maclaren and Cobb respectively moved and seconded an amendment allowing contracting out, if the employer contributed enough to the insurance fund to pay for adequate compensation in all cases of injury or death, and if, in a secret ballot vote administered by the Board of Trade, two thirds of the workmen concerned expressed themselves to be in favor of the system and desirous of contracting out. Again the two took the argument of the L&NWRR, but this time they had more powerful ammunition: they announced that a secret ballot had been given to the employees of that company, whereupon 90 per cent had expressed a preference for the present system instead of that proposd by the bill. Theatrically Maclaren pointed out the hardships the workers would suffer if they lost their insurance funds, then concluded his argument by referring to an exchange of letters between himself and the Member from Battersea (Mr.

24. Parliamentary Debates, Fourth Series, *18,* 457.

Burns) in a prominent newspaper. In this exchange Burns had strongly objected to the Friendly Societies, "because he thinks they are antagonistic to Trade Unions, and are Union-smashing agencies."[25] This, according to Maclaren, accounted for the unions' opposition to the otherwise beneficial system of contracting out.

Asquith countered with arguments about the danger of the worker making improvident contracts and, in the long run, the certain frustration of one of the aims of the bill—to provide an incentive against negligence—which contracting out would cause.

Asquith's arguments were systematically countered during the course of the debate over Maclaren's amendment. The debate lasted for three nights and became more and more heated as the House neared a division. On the night of the division (10 November) the party Whips feverishly mustered every available Member, on both sides, and when the results were announced the Government had carried its negative to the amendment by a scant eighteen votes.[26] Clearly, since during the seven evenings devoted to consideration of the bill no other issue occupied the House's attention for more than a few speeches, contracting out was considered the central issue. The Government's narrow margin (they had a working majority of forty) reflects the division of opinion even within their own ranks.

Chamberlain had been abroad during the debate on the Maclaren amendment, else the results of the division might have been different. He returned in time to make a speech on 23 November before the third reading was passed. Announcing at the outset that he intended to support the bill because it extended the benefits of the 1880 Act to all classes of workers, he maintained nonetheless that the bill was inadequate in scope and mischievous in conception: inadequate because it did not take into account well over half of the nation's industrial accidents, and mischievous because its prohibition of contracting out would block the further development of those institutions designed to take care of all

25. Ibid., p. 489.
26. Ibid., p. 756.

accidents, the Friendly Societies. How, he went on to ask, could the imposition of liability in a case where control did not exist possibly tend to the exercise of greater care? Would the least favored workman be induced to exercise greater care by the knowledge that his employer was liable for his negligence?[27]

Asquith, who was reduced to acrimony and *argumentum ad hominem* for his reply, sneered at Chamberlain's absence during the report stage, his subsequent return, and his presumption in then telling the House how badly it had mismanaged its affairs. In this, the most dramatic confrontation between the two men, Asquith clearly lost the field to Chamberlain; during the remainder of his speech he failed to counter a single one of the latter's arguments. By that time, however, such a failure went unnoticed: the Opposition had nearly deserted the House, and the third reading passed, as expected, without a division.[28]

But opposition of a more prophetic order followed the third reading, for as soon as the Speaker would recognize them, twenty-one Members rose one after another to either protest the bill or request that it be amended "in another place" (the House of Lords) so as to permit contracting out.

As mentioned above, Asquith received a flood of letters from alarmed businessmen as soon as his speech on the second reading (20 February) was published in the newspapers. Included in the rush came one from the Managing Director of the Oldbury Alkali Company, Alexander M. Chance, urging him to reconsider his position on contracting out for all the reasons already discussed. It is interesting to note that Chance also forwarded a copy of his letter to Chamberlain, who, had he not already known the arguments, certainly thereby had them given ready to hand. Asquith answered Chance with the usual assurances, and there their correspondence terminated.[29]

The second reading of the Employers' Liability Bill in the House

27. Ibid., p. 1560.
28. Ibid., p. 1585.
29. PRO, H.O. 45/9865/B13816/14.

of Lords was scheduled for 30 November; before the debate formally began, Lord Knutsworth presented a petition from the employees of the Oldbury Alkali Company requesting that contracting out be permitted if the contract obtained the approval of the Board of Trade or some other such Government agency.[30] The Marquess of Ripon (Secretary of State for the Colonies) then moved the second reading; Ripon's speech amounted to no more than a paraphrase in less rhetorical form of Asquith's on 20 February.

As in the House of Commons, the Lords never debated the wisdom of the total abolition of the doctrine of common employment. The Earl of Dudley followed Ripon in debate, perfunctorily gave his approval of the abolition of the doctrine, and remarked that "The additional liability would be largely covered by insurance, the cost of which would eventually be embodied in the price of the product."[31] Common employment, therefore, would be swept away, with all its hardships, at the cost of a small tax on the consumer—an excellent and cheap method of disposing of a rankling grievance.

The Earl of Dudley owned several coal mines and employed approximately 3,000 men to work them. Having stated his approval of the abolition of the doctrine of common employment, he went on to state his categorical opposition to the clause forbidding contracting out. It had been his case (*Griffiths v. Earl of Dudley*) which had made the practice legal in 1881. Under the proposed law he estimated that he would save upward of £325 per year if he insured against his liabilities and discontinued his contributions to the Friendly Societies. Remarking that he saw no reason for employers to "stand up to be shot at from both sides," he went on to deplore the deleterious effects which the proposed legislation would have on the morale of the workers, the financial loss they would inevitably suffer, and the crippling effects on industry of a worsened employer-employee relationship. He recapitulated the

30. Parliamentary Debates, Fourth Series, *19*, 53.
31. Ibid., pp. 63–68.

evidence of the secret ballot given to the men of the L&NWRR, and indicated that identical results had been obtained by a similar poll of his own men. In conclusion, having summed up his evidence, he moved that some amendment permitting contracting out be inserted in the bill.

The Duke of Argyll, the Marquess of Londonderry, Lord Stalbridge, and the Earl of Selbourne all followed suit with arguments in support of contracting out. The debate was adjourned and resumed again on 8 December, at which time Dudley moved the amendment subsequently adopted: contracting out to be permitted if, in a secret ballot administered by the Board of Trade subsequent to the passage of the bill, the majority of workers wanted it; such an agreement between employer and employed must provide adequate compensation in all cases of injury; the employer must contribute to the fund; and the whole contract would have to be approved by the Board of Trade. The Earl of Denbigh succeeded in having the workers' vote raised to a two-thirds majority, and on 12 December the amended bill passed the second reading. On 14 December, with an added amendment providing that the employer's contribution to the fund should be no less than one quarter that of the worker, the bill passed the third reading and the Lords sent it back to the House of Commons.[32]

Just as Chamberlain, the leader of the Opposition in the House of Commons, had played a large role in the debate on the bill, so also had Salisbury, the leader of the Opposition in the House of Lords. The critical difference lay in Salisbury's undoubted control of an overwhelming majority, for, as we have seen, all but a handful of peers left Gladstone over Home Rule. With the passage of the bill in Commons, those in favor of contracting out placed their hopes on the House of Lords. Salisbury naturally became the target for deputations, and on 4 December the Miners' Permanent Relief Society sent a delegation to urge upon him the advisability of a contracting-out clause. The usual flurry of scandalous attacks upon

32. Ibid., p. 781.

the credentials of the delegation ensued: Asquith announced in
Commons on 12 December that he had recently received a resolution from the Miners' Federation of Great Britain which disallowed
the authority of the delegation to represent the views of the miners
and which urged the Government to resist the insertion of the
Dudley amendment.[33] On 19 December Mr. Tomlinson angrily
inquired whether Asquith was aware that at the meeting of the
Miners' Permanent Relief Society on 16 December it was unanimously resolved that the Miners' Federation of Great Britain
had no authority to speak on behalf of their society (of whose
59,000 members only a fraction belonged to the Federation), and
that the deputation which had waited upon Salisbury had been
fully authorized.[34]

Asquith opened the debate in Commons on the Lords' amendments and moved that they be rejected out of hand. He briefly
recapitulated the argument from inequality of bargaining power,
then attacked the machinery set up by the amendment for determining whether a contract should be allowed. Chamberlain, who
followed immediately, charged him with quibbling over detail
and neglecting to argue the principle of the amendment. This
Chamberlain proceeded to do. Most forcefully he rephrased his
argument about safety:

> You cannot induce the employer to take greater precautions
> by punishing him for accidents over which any precautions he
> may take will have absolutely no influence whatsoever. . . .
> And that is all that the Bill does. . . . If you think you are
> going to make the workman more careful by punishing his
> employer you are very much mistaken.[35]

Urging that the House not reject the Lords' amendment, he argued
that the employers would only be able to contract themselves out
of the Act by undertaking liabilities and responsibilities which

33. Ibid., p. 1167.
34. Ibid., p. 1760.
35. Ibid., 20, 2–14.

were greater than those imposed upon them by the law. Since Asquith had stated categorically that the Government would not accept the bill as amended, Chamberlain accused him of "seeking a cry against the House of Lords."[36] In this contention he was supported by Tomlinson, who remarked that Asquith" seemed to have two objects before him—one to set employers against employed, and the other to set one House of Parliament against the other."[37] In any case Asquith won his point, for when the division was taken the House rejected the Dudley amendment 213 to 157.

The subsequent history of the quarrel is complicated and irrelevant. Suffice it to say that the final compromise measure, which would have permitted existing arrangements to remain in effect for three more years before finally being terminated, passed the House on 13 February 1894 by the rather narrow margin of two votes (215 to 213) only to be rejected by the House of Lords 23 to 137 on 19 February 1894. On the principle of permitting contracting out the House of Lords refused to budge. But they bent over backward to meet the objections of the Government: they eventually raised the contribution by the employer from one quarter to one third; they inserted a clause permitting the workman to release himself from the contract whenever he wished; they provided that, in the event the fund proved inadequate and the employer refused to guarantee it, then the contract would not stand in bar of recovery; and finally they inserted a further amendment that contracting out was never to be a condition of service. Asquith likewise stood firm, and, of course, so did the representatives of organized labor. On 13 February 1894, Burns spoke for the Trades Union Council in the House:

> With regard to the Amendment of Lord Dudley in another place, if that is carried, contracting out will be universally extended, and many of the Unions connected with the Organizations of unskilled laborers will no longer be able to

36. Ibid., p. 18.
37. Ibid., p. 31.

exist. . . . The real object of the masters in promoting the mutual insurance schemes is to prejudice the workmen, to damage the friendly societies, and to injure the cause of Trade Unionism.[38]

This position seems to have been clearly recognized by both sides, for on 29 January, Salisbury, speaking in the House of Lords, had remarked that

the refusal of the Government even to give us reasons for the somewhat overbearing course they have pursued proves to us that they are not acting on their own instincts or in obedience to the motives which naturally guide them in dealing with the Members of both Houses of Parliament, but that they are the victims of a dire necessity and the slaves of a cruel organization.[39]

The final chapter in the story of the 1893 Employers' Liability Bill occurred on 20 February 1894 when Gladstone, not Asquith, rose to move that the order for consideration of the Lords' amendments be dropped, thus effectively killing the bill. Gladstone severely castigated the Lords for their insistence upon contracting out, and rejected the idea because

it will tend by a subtle, but a most extended, operation of causes too efficient in their nature to impair that position of independence and self-action on the part of the working man in the face of his employer which it is essential for the benefit of both that he should always be able to hold.[40]

Chamberlain responded with a speech bitterly condemning the Government for throwing their bill away on a minor point, for refusing to compromise, and for seeking a cry against the House of Lords. He then disowned any further responsibility toward the bill and led a mass exodus of Liberal Unionists and Conservatives

38. Ibid., *21*, 439–40.
39. Ibid., *20*, 1627.
40. Ibid., *21*, 858.

from the House, leaving the Liberals to kill their own bill by a vote of 225 to 6.[41]

Some idea of the complexity of conflicting motives should emerge from the brief history given above. Most historians, if they consider the Employers' Liability Bill at all, see in its failure further evidence that during this period the House of Lords blindly exercised its powers in a purely partisan fashion, wrecking or mutilating any legislation sent for its consideration by the Liberals. Such was the view adopted by Gladstone, bitter over the failure of his pet Irish Home Rule Bill, and though unsupported by the facts it has nonetheless achieved a surprisingly wide currency. To attribute the action of the House of Lords to partisan motives is no more true in the case of Home Rule than in the case of Employers' Liability. While clearly Salisbury commanded an overwhelming majority in the House of Lords, it cannot be too strongly emphasized that this majority dated from 1886 and arose solely out of thoughtful (or impassioned) opposition to Gladstone's expressed intention of granting autonomy to Ireland. On that issue the Whig peerage deserted Gladstone, and this desertion cannot be attributed to "party" motives. Why should the Lords' subsequent and entirely predictable opposition to the Home Rule Bill be attributed to "partisan" motives?

On the question of the Employers' Liability Bill, the House of Lords may have known that their insistence upon the inclusion of a contracting-out clause would lead the Government to reject the amended bill. But they made every conceivable concession short of allowing the prohibition of contracting out; they spared no efforts to meet the objections of the Government. No one has attributed Chamberlain's support of the Dudley amendment to unthinking partisan behavior; it should be perfectly clear that he acted on the basis of his own stated convictions. Why is it not permissible to allow that Salisbury and the House of Lords also acted upon their own convictions? In any event the election returns in 1895 sug-

41. Ibid., 20, 899.

gest that the people of England did not accept Gladstone's interpretation of the House of Lords' behavior: the Conservatives and
Liberal Unionists took over the Government with the second
largest majority of the nineteenth century, and had it not been
for the loyal support of the Celtic Fringe the Liberal party would
have disappeared altogether.

We can sort out the various motives at work on the Employers'
Liability Bill. Both parties were committed to an extension of the
employers' liability; this is evident from their expressed intentions,
from the total absence of any opposition to the clause disallowing
the defense of common employment, and from the uncontested
passage of the bill's second reading in both Houses. The real controversy centered about the prohibition of contracting out. Were
contracting out to be prohibited, the employers in the House of
Lords (e.g. the Earl of Dudley) saw themselves threatened with a
mass of litigation and all the normally attendant ill-feeling. And
for the injured workman such a system offered little chance of
remuneration. Chamberlain and the Marquess of Salisbury thought
that the bill would not do what the Government claimed it would
do (inspire the employer to exercise greater care in the conduct
of his business), and objected therefore to removing those conditions under which the certain system of compensation for the inevitable disasters of industry had grown up. The labor unions,
while arguing from the Government's theory of safety and accident
prevention, saw quite clearly that contracting out, in as impersonal
a system of industry as that growing up in England, held enormous
dangers for the unassisted workman; the unions saw that labor, in
order to avoid exploitation, must in a sense be united against the
employers, and that in the long run it would be to the worker's
advantage to avoid entangling arrangements with his employer;
they preferred—rightly—autonomy with its attendant strong bargaining position to mutual arrangements (no matter how immediately beneficial) which carried encumbrances to unfettered
collective action. Gladstone's sole interest in the Employers' Liability Bill stemmed from what he construed to be the mutilation of

the bill by the Lords. Gladstone sought a cry to the country, the people versus the peers, and hoped thereby to overcome the Lords' rejection of his Home Rule Bill.[42] His position and the position of his Government seem to have been determined by the labor unions, whose support they desperately needed. Among the workmen themselves no clear consensus emerged on either side of the argument.

Finally, the position of Asquith needs explication. In the first place, Asquith formulated the Government's position in opposing contracting out, and having done so stuck to it with unflinching tenacity despite the certain knowledge that the House of Lords would insist on altering that position. Nothing if not a practical man, such stubbornness appears unreasonable, for it meant the certain failure of the bill. That he would have adopted such a position and refused to budge from it solely upon the request of the labor union representatives is on the face of it an inadequate explanation, for Asquith certainly knew of the dichotomy of opinion on the subject within the ranks of labor itself. But this is not to deny for a second that he relied heavily on the support of the labor representatives to maintain his position once adopted.

Rather the explanation lies with his principles. In order to better understand them it is instructive to turn for a moment to another stage of his public career. In 1906, as Chancellor of the Exchequer in Campbell-Bannerman's Government, Asquith found his principles directly challenged by the Prime Minister as well as labor. The issue centered around the Trades Dispute Bill. Briefly, a recent court decision had opened union funds to suits for damages arising out of the unauthorized and illegal activities of members of a trade union engaged in a strike or other dispute. If the trade unions were to survive, clearly they could not be made financially accountable for the malicious or otherwise culpable behavior of their members. On this point all were agreed; the means by which to achieve the needed protection were disputed.

42. Magnus, *Gladstone: A Biography,* p. 419.

Campbell-Bannerman felt that if the object was to render trade union funds immune, the law should come right out and say so. In this he was supported by the trade unions, who took a dim view of Asquith's proposal. The latter wished to so alter and restrict the law of agency in its application to trade unions that the same object could be obtained without including in the statute words which gave to one class a privilege not shared by others. Campbell-Bannerman's view prevailed; but not before Asquith had secured the inclusion of the phrase italicized below with the threat to resign if his request was refused:

> An action against a Trade Union, *whether of workmen or masters,* or against any members or officials thereof, on behalf of themselves and all other members of the Trade Union in respect of any tortious act alleged to have been committed by or on behalf of the Trade Union, shall not be entertained by any court.[43]

Thus, in the words of an Asquith biographer, "he had a determined hostility to giving a specially privileged legal position to any group."[44] Asquith's position derived directly from T. H. Green, and from the orthodox Liberal position before him. Green writes,

> Everyone has an interest in securing to everyone else the free use and enjoyment and disposal of his possessions, so long as that freedom on the part of one does not interfere with a like freedom on the part of others, because such freedom contributes to that equal development of the faculties of all which is the highest good for all.[45]

It is unnecessary to search further. Asquith, in his speech on the second reading, indicated that he hoped to remove an anomalous exception to the law: the defense of common employment. He intended to streamline the law by remedial, not preferential, legis-

43. Spender and Asquith, *Life of Herbert Henry Asquith,* I, 182.
44. Jenkins, *Asquith,* p. 171.
45. Richter, *The Politics of Conscience,* p. 284.

lation—a basic distinction. He did not want any exceptions in the law which would give preferred treatment to a specific class of persons, and accordingly he opposed both the defense of common employment (which put employers in an exceptional position) and the Dudley amendment (which put the employees in the exceptional position of being able to break their contracts). Most emphatically he did not want a clause that provided for governmental approval of anyone's contracts. How much tidier and more logical to forbid such contracts altogether!

Asquith's position in opposing contracting out rested on the quite simple and correct belief that such contracts could be dangerous to the workmen, and therefore required safeguards—again, preferential legislation. In this belief, once again he was supported by T. H. Green. As it happens, Green wrote an essay on "Liberal Legislation and Freedom of Contract" in which he specifically discussed the Employers' Liability Bill of 1880, and took violent exception to the practice of contracting out:

> To uphold the sanctity of contracts is doubtless a prime business of government, but it is no less its business to provide against contracts being made which from the helplessness of one of the parties to them, instead of being a security for freedom, become an instrument of disguised oppression.[46]

Chapter 5 ends the discussion of what did not happen: the 1893 Employers' Liability Bill did not pass, and the issue did not get settled. But all the alternatives save that suggested by Chamberlain had been attempted, and clearly the situation could not rest where it lay: commitments in time, effort, and conviction had been made in too great abundance by both sides. From this point the accumulated progression of events had to lead inevitably to Workmen's Compensation.

46. Thomas Hill Green, *Liberal Legislation and Freedom of Contract* (Oxford, Slatter and Rose, 1881), p. 14.

CHAPTER 6

Workmen's Compensation Act of 1897

After the failure of the 1893 Employers' Liability Bill no one ever
again seriously attempted that approach to solving the problem
of industrial accidents. To anyone who cared to look, the hand-
writing on the wall announced the eventual solution in the form
of Chamberlain's proposed amendment to the second reading of
the 1893 bill, namely, workmen's compensation. No other alternatives existed. The present chapter deals briefly with the inevitable
denouement of the situation: first, the total collapse of the Liberals
and the decisive victory of the Unionists at the polls in 1895; then
the character and beliefs which motivated the two leaders of the
Unionist alliance; finally, the uncontested passage of the Workmen's Compensation Act of 1897.

On 1 March 1894, in what turned out to be his last speech in
the House of Commons, Gladstone bitterly denounced the House
of Lords for what he construed to be their purely partisan behavior
toward all legislation sent to them by the Liberals. He warned that
the continued exercise of their powers in such a fashion would result in the overthrow of their House. Perhaps the partial fulfill-
ment of his prophecy in 1911 (when the powers of the upper
House were in fact severely curtailed) has led historians to accept
uncritically his analysis of the events in 1894. However that may
be, Gladstone resigned as Prime Minister two days after delivering
his final speech, and the Queen, thankful to be rid of him, promptly
and on her own responsibility summoned Lord Rosebery to head
the Liberal Government.

Since the Liberals' already slight majority had begun to dwindle
rapidly, and since, with the departure of Gladstone, their leadership was paralyzed by internal power struggles, it probably was of
small consequence whom the Queen chose for her Prime Minister:

any Liberal Government was doomed to failure. But the choice of
Rosebery insured that that failure would be unmitigated.

Rosebery had entered politics by going straight to the House
of Lords, and accordingly had had no experience in the rough and
tumble of the House of Commons. That fact, coupled with his
almost feminine sensitivity to criticism, made it very difficult for
him to command any respect from the Commons. In addition he
had merged his own enormous estates with those of Hanna
Rothschild (an only daughter and heiress), thus becoming one
of the wealthiest men in England; furthermore Rosebery kept a
stable of superb thoroughbreds, and his horses won the Derby
both years of his prime ministership. Such achievements could
scarcely be calculated to secure for him the support of the strong
Nonconformist element in his own party in the Commons.
Similarly, his hold upon the affections of the House of Lords could
scarcely have been more slender, for he had held that body in lifelong contempt and made no effort to conceal it. When addressing
the House of Lords, "Rosebery adopted the tone of a very con-
sciously sane chaplain addressing the inmates of a home for
imbeciles."[1] On 7 April 1894 he sent the Queen a long and lucid
Memorandum on the subject of the House of Lords, in which he
adopted Gladstone's view of their "scandalous" behavior; the
Queen indignantly rejected such an interpretation and it seems
Rosebery lost some of her confidence as well.

In addition to these political disadvantages, Rosebery had personal disabilities as well. He had no patience with petty vexations,
and he never had been able to bring himself to do anything he did
not want to do. When confronted with unpleasantness, his wealth
had always allowed him simply to withdraw. Winston Churchill
wrote of him:

> As the franchise broadened and the elegant, glittering, im-
> posing trappings faded from British Parliamentary and public

1. Robert Rhodes James, *Rosebery* (London, Weidenfeld and Nicholson,
1963), p. 75.

life, Lord Rosebery was conscious of an ever-widening gap between himself and the Radical electorate . . . one had to face the caucus, the wire-puller and the soapbox; one had to stand on platforms built of planks of all descriptions. He did not like it. He could not do it . . . He would not stoop; he did not conquer.[2]

Beginning with his "dominant partner" speech (which thoroughly alienated the Irish, for he stated that Home Rule would never be realized without the consent of England, "the dominant partner,") Rosebery's administration failed as disastrously as might be expected.[3] It is only surprising that it lasted as long as it did. All through the remainder of 1894 and 1895 the Government vacillated, hedged, accomplished almost nothing, fulminated against the peers, and refrained from any engagement. All the while their majority steadily dwindled and the country became more and more impatient. The attitude of the Government was that it longed to expire but would neither resign nor go to the polls.[4] Eventually, on 21 June 1895, the Government was caught off guard, defeated by a snap vote taken on the Army estimates, and Rosebery resigned. Salisbury formed a Government, Parliament was dissolved on July 8, and in the general election which followed the Liberal party suffered an overwhelming defeat.

During the Rosebery Administration the Liberals had pursued a policy which they dubbed "filling up the cup." Their intention was to pass measures whose merits were self-evident and to allow the House of Lords to destroy them, hoping thereby to arouse the country to anger against the peers. The difficulty was that, if such merit existed at all, it was not evident to the country, and the Opposition facetiously dubbed it a policy of "ploughing the sands." In endeavoring to "fill up the cup," the Liberals stuck doggedly by their Newcastle Program, which, as Rosebery later

2. Ibid., p. 223.
3. Marriott, *Modern England 1885–1932*, p. 72.
4. Garvin, *Chamberlain*, 2, 635.

admitted, succeeded only in alienating every important interest in the country.[5] The Conservatives and Liberal Unionists made great political capital out of the failures of the Liberals, most particularly over the Home Rule and the Employers' Liability bills. The latter became the dominant battle cry of the Unionists (as both parties came to be called): Chamberlain's slogan during the preelection campaign was "A Compensation Act for workmen, irrespective of cause of accident."[6]

Chamberlain's campaign got under way in the late summer of 1894. He had begun to prepare the way for a formal alliance with the Conservatives as early as 1892. In November of that year he wrote in a popular periodical, *Nineteenth Century,* that "In social questions the Conservatives have always been more progressive than the Liberals, and in their latest legislation have only returned to the old Tory Tradition."[7]

On 11 October 1894 he addressed his constituents at the Birmingham Town Hall on the subject of workmen's compensation, saying that the victims of industrial accidents must be regarded as "the wounded soldiers of industry."

> In my opinion, not now for the first time expressed, the cost of every accident in every employment is rightly a first charge on the cost of production. . . . We may fairly call upon [the Government] to leave off these perpetual constitutional experiments [referring to Home Rule] and to use its vast resource and its great influence to promote some practical measures to secure the greatest happiness of the greatest number.[8]

He campaigned along the same lines within the ranks of the Conservative party itself: in a letter to Sir Henry James, dated 11 December 1894, he wrote,

> a Unionist Government should from the outset declare its settled intention to leave all questions of constitutional re-

5. James, p. 385.
6. Garvin, 2, 608.
7. Ibid.
8. Ibid., p. 609.

form and change of machinery entirely alone for the present and to devote itself entirely to the study and prosecution of social legislation.[9]

Anyone who had heard or read the debates in the House of Lords on the Employers' Liability Bill would have known that at least on that subject Chamberlain and Salisbury saw exactly eye to eye. Both men had made virtually identical comments on the bill and both proposed identical solutions to the problem: on 8 December 1893 Salisbury stated,

> If I could have my way I should like to see insurance made universal on the principle on which these agreements [contracting out] are drawn—namely, that it should apply to all accidents to whatever cause they are due—whether they are due to the negligence of the men or not—and I would gladly see the State giving its aid in order to provide the machinery for carrying such [a law] into effect.[10]

On 20 December 1893 Chamberlain, replying to Asquith, said,

> Even now I should be glad to see some general and universal system carried out, extending to every workman . . . [failing that] then the next best thing is to give every facility for the making of mutual arrangements, and if they prove to be so popular as to be widely adopted, what remains to be provided for by legislation will be very small indeed.[11]

If any doubt still remained as to the intention of the two men, it was dispelled by a publicized letter from Chamberlain to Salisbury dated 29 October 1894 entitled "Memorandum of a Program of Social Reform." In the course of the memorandum Chamberlain stated that "above all, regarding a full system of compensation to workmen for accidents, it is most desirable in the interests of the Unionist party that this question should be finally settled."[12]

9. Ibid., p. 618.
10. Parliamentary Debates, Fourth Series, *19*, 781.
11. Ibid., *20, 27*.
12. Garvin, *2, 616*.

Salisbury publicly acquiesced to the proposals contained in the letter.

Thus, when the Conservatives went to the polls, their leadership was solidly united on basic issues. The direction they would follow if elected could not have been more obvious. But quite a different situation prevailed with the Liberals, whose leadership was hopelessly divided: for Sir William Harcourt, the ex-Chancellor of the Exchequer, the issue upon which he asked his constituency for a mandate was local veto on the sale of alcoholic beverages; they refused to reelect him. For John Morley, the ex-Chief Secretary for Ireland, Home Rule led the way, and he also lost his seat in the House. As for Lord Rosebery, if he said anything at all he confined his remarks to fulminating about the House of Lords; two years after the election he retired from politics altogether. In 1895 the Conservatives swept into office with the largest majority held by either party since 1832.[13] Depending on which way the Irish vote swung, in any division the Unionists controlled an absolute majority ranging in size from 152 to 316. The country had returned a total of 411 Unionists, 177 Liberals, and of course 82 Irish Members. England evidently had tired of ineffective government.

Despite Salisbury's wish that Chamberlain take either the Home Office or the Exchequer, Chamberlain surprised everyone by opting for the Colonial Office. It would have made no difference which post Chamberlain accepted, for he and Salisbury were the acknowledged leaders of the Unionist Government. Despite their wholly disparate backgrounds, the two men managed to work in complete harmony. Salisbury had retained the Foreign Office for himself, and for that reason it was essential that they see eye to eye, at least in foreign affairs. In domestic affairs, Salisbury publicly announced that Chamberlain spoke for the Unionist Government,[14] and in

13. All based on H. Whates, *The Third Salisbury Administration* (London, Vacker and Sons, 1900), pp. 12–17.

14. "Salisbury replied to all whom it might concern, that on social questions 'Mr. Chamberlain is the spokesman of our party.'" Garvin, *3*, 158.

this way avoided even the possibility of friction. But he did more than merely relinquish the realm of domestic affairs to Chamberlain: he also backed Chamberlain to the hilt in whatever social legislation the latter proposed. The most striking example of that is Salisbury's vigorous support for the Workmen's Compensation Act. Considering his reputation for being a stern and inflexible Conservative, such behavior seems at first glance out of character; but a closer look at his background explains how he and Chamberlain could work so well together.

Robert Cecil, Marquis of Salisbury, was born to the tradition that children of wealthy families should show interest in and feel responsibility for the welfare of those who were born in less favorable circumstances.[15] His mind was independent and rigorously logical, and though afflicted with frail health he had an enormous capacity for sustained work. He was, in short, an outstanding exception in a family "the general mediocrity of whose intelligence was only varied by instances of quite exceptional stupidity."[16] Eminently conservative throughout his life, he nonetheless was possessed of a demonstrated capacity for compromise. He modeled his political deportment on his two idols, Pitt and Castlereagh. He admired the former's moderation; he admired the latter's unbending indifference to awards, popularity, and acclaim coupled with a determination to do what his selfless honesty dictated to be right.[17] Probably because he gave his personal views with sometimes appalling frankness, he was enormously popular with the people, who saw in him a man of scrupulous honestry and unflinching integrity.

He demonstrated his willingness to sacrifice self and career for his principles in his dispute with Disraeli over household suffrage in the Reform Bill of 1867.[18] Feeling that the Government's

15. A. L. Kennedy, *Salisbury 1830–1903, Portrait of a Statesman* (London, John Murray Publishers, 1953), p. 37.
16. Lady Gwendolen Cecil, *Salisbury, I, 1.*
17. Kennedy, pp. 38–41.
18. Ibid., p. 142.

position was morally reprehensible in view of their earlier stand, he resigned rather than remain in office under those circumstances. He subsequently came to accept the Reform Bill (as witness his close association and work with Disraeli from 1874 to 1880) in all its implications, and remarked in a speech in the House of Lords shortly after Disraeli's death that "Our absolute sovereign is the people of this country."[19] Oddly, though Disraeli showed the greater trust in the British people, the people came to trust Salisbury in a way they had never trusted Disraeli.

In early life Salisbury was much concerned with the rights of property. He vigorously opposed a graduated income tax coupled to an extension of the franchise because "the combined effect would be to bring an ultimate divorce between power and responsibility"; and in fact the time would come when "the rich will pay all the taxes and the poor will make all the laws." He foresaw in 1867 with alarm but singular clarity the day when "labour gives law to capital, Trades Unions rule supreme, democratic Parliaments contrive a graduated income tax, [with] the poor voting supplies and the rich finding ways and means." Salisbury's pejorative use of the word "democracy" must be understood in the context of the times: by "democracy" Salisbury meant (as did most people) mob rule—"To give," he remarked, "the guidance of this intricate machinery of Government to the least instructed class in the community, is to adopt in the management of the Empire principles which would not be entertained for a moment in any other department of human affairs."[20]

Six years of working hand in glove with Disraeli (1874–80) softened his attitude. He came to agree more and more with the Prime Minister's ideas of social reform, and worked hard for the latter's Public Health Act of 1875. Salisbury was thoroughly sympathetic to Disraeli's maxim that all government exists solely for the good of the governed; that those who are possessed of

19. Ibid., p. 141.
20. Ibid., pp. 34, 60.

public power are trustees, not for their own class but for the nation. In a speech at Edinburgh in 1882 he declared that the Conservative party was and ought to be forward in defense of the poor: "No system that is not just as between rich and poor can hope to survive," he declared.[21] And for just this reason Salisbury entertained a strong suspicion of class-conscious radicals who, he thought, were fomenting a dangerous breach among the people. He accused those who led the poorer classes of

> industriously impressing upon them that the function of legislation is to transfer to them something from the pockets of their more fortunate fellow-countrymen; and it is too much to hope that a doctrine, which teaches that a disregard of the Tenth Commandment is the highest duty of citizenship, should not gradually impress itself on the minds to which it is addressed.

But he was entirely willing to countenance change: "The object of our party is not, and ought not to be, simply to keep things as they are. In the first place the enterprise is impossible. In the next place, there is much in our present mode of thought and action which it is highly undesirable to conserve."[22]

Salisbury, throughout his life, believed that those who had had "advantages" were under a special obligation to perform public service. Having had leisure for thought and study he considered it their task to lead and direct society. He demanded of this ruling class absolute standards of character—devotion, energy, integrity and self-sacrifice—and denounced in scathing language the "smart set" of his day, whom he held in utter contempt. For all his hatred of injustice Salisbury never led any crusades for reform. He contented himself with supporting the reforming efforts of others. Enormous injustices did in fact exist and were being silently borne; his most recent biographer writes, "It is the abiding blemish in

21. Ibid., p. 144.
22. Ibid., pp. 145, 146.

Lord Salisbury's record that he did not take the first opportunity to investigate them."[23]

Predictably, therefore, though Salisbury concerned himself mainly with the conduct of foreign affairs during his third Government, he gladly supported the reforms suggested by Chamberlain. And certainly it would have come as a great surprise if Chamberlain had not pushed for reforms, given the opportunity to do so. Once he had entered politics, his background dictated the role of reformer: he came from a Liberal Nonconformist family where dissent from established institutions was traditional.

Chamberlain was born in 1836 into a London family which had successfully engaged in the business of shoemaking. Of distinctly middle-class origins, therefore, his family also identified itself with the Liberal party and the Unitarian church. His father insisted that the family devote a certain amount of time each week to the discussion of public affairs; he also took an active interest, as did many Nonconformists, in welfare work through his church. From a comparatively early age young Chamberlain was expected not only to teach Sunday School to slum children but also to assist in exhorting slum dwellers to adopt Victorian attitudes about cleanliness, godliness, industry, thrift and self-control. He early had drummed into him the Unitarian belief that "the Fatherhood of God implies the brotherhood of Man," and that "Right conduct is positive and demands personal good works." According to Garvin, such an early background and training accounted for not only his lifelong concern with social reform but also his Nonconformist instinct for assailing things usually accepted.[24]

Chamberlain had gone to school for only eight years when he left at the age of sixteen to work in his father's shoemaking business. He stayed there for two years as an ordinary workman, becoming familiar with the attitude and outlook of labor at first hand. In 1854 he left London to work in his uncle's wood screw factory in Birmingham; his father, who had put up part of the

23. Ibid., pp. 194, 196.
24. Garvin, *1*, 16–44.

capital for the new undertaking, wanted someone in Birmingham to look after his interests. At this young Chamberlain proved highly adept, for he had great business acumen. In fact it was largely owing to his direction that the concern of Nettleford and Chamberlain proved as successful as it did.

The details of Chamberlain's early political career need not concern us here. Suffice it to say that when he eventually did become interested in politics his rise to prominence was meteoric. His three-year term as Mayor of Birmingham, which began in 1873, brought him national recognition, for during that term, as he himself said, the city was "parked, paved, assized, marketed, gas-and-watered."[25] In 1876 he gave up both the firm of Nettlefold and Chamberlain and the mayoralty of Birmingham, in order to represent his adopted city in Parliament. Within four years he had achieved sufficient prominence to be included in Gladstone's Government as President of the Board of Trade.

Though a Liberal by birth and early training, Chamberlain was never partisan for party's sake; his allegiance fell to whichever party seemed most likely to achieve his legislative ends. By 1885 those ends did not include any further "constitutional experiments" in Ireland. In fact, as early as 1873 Chamberlain condemned Gladstone and his Liberal colleagues because they either did not or would not see that the social question henceforth must dominate and overshadow all politics. In an explosive article written for the September 1873 issue of the *Fortnightly Review* (then edited by John Morley) he remarked that "The unexampled commercial prosperity of the last few years has led many to lose sight of the coexisting misery and discontent of a large portion of the population . . . whose homes would disgrace a barbarous country."[26]

Dating from the Reform Bill of 1868, Chamberlain entertained a strong suspicion that one could expect more social reform from the Tory party, which was not so encumbered with the laissez-faire doctrines of the Manchester School; he certainly recognized,

25. Evans, *The Victorian Age, 1815–1914*, p. 338.
26. Garvin, *I*, 159.

admired, and eventually made use of that humanitarian spirit awakened by Disraeli and carried on by Lord Randolph Churchill.[27] When, finally, his convictions about the integrity of Great Britain precluded any further cooperation with Gladstone, Chamberlain unhesitatingly made the break.

To try to fit Joseph Chamberlain into the category of Tory Democrat serves no purpose; suffice it to say that during the 1890s Chamberlain's position as leader of the left wing of the Unionist party was undisputed; but by the end of the third Salisbury Government he was far better known as an imperialist and a tariff reformer than as a social reformer.

But before imperialism caught his fancy, social reform was his chief passion. A complete statement of his position on the labor question appears in a contribution to the *Nineteenth Century* in November 1892, in which he elucidated an eight-point program, headed by a recommendation to reduce the workday to eight hours. In 1892 a bill to shorten the miners' working day to eight hours was introduced, and Chamberlain supported it. In the debate Chamberlain bitterly attacked the exponents of laissez-faire, and provided a most interesting clue to his own beliefs:

> It [the Eight Hour Bill] does extend the functions of the State, and I want to know whether there is any one really nowadays who is prepared to abide by the strict doctrine of laissez-faire, which perhaps twenty years ago was accepted as preferable to that other doctrine of constant niggling and unreasonable and imprudent interference which preceded it. Nowadays the doctrine is a much wiser one. It avoids the extreme of continual and impertinent interference on the one hand, but deems it the duty of the State to interfere when it can do so for the good of the community. My idea of the true doctrine is expressed in the words of a political economist, who certainly is not a Socialist, or an extreme man in ordinary matters—Professor Jevons. Professor Jevons says that the

27. Gulley, *Joseph Chamberlain and English Social Politics*, p. 327.

State is justified in passing any law, or even in doing any single act which, in its ulterior consequences, adds to the sum total of happiness. I accept the doctrine of Professor Jevons.[28]

In the passage just cited Chamberlain referred to W. Stanley Jevons, at that time an economist of sufficient stature to carry weight in any argument. Chamberlain drew his quotation from Jevons' book entitled *The State in Relation to Labour,* which had first been published in 1882 and had gone through three editions by 1894.[29] Jevons' argument amounts to no more than a logical extension of utilitarian thought to its extreme position, and implicit in it are all the problems confronting the utilitarians: where can one find legislators sufficiently expert to accurately foresee all the consequences of their legislation? And how does one get around the virtual impossibility of defining "good" without reference to some external a priori system? Particularly with reference to the last question, Jevons burned his own bridges. His entire writing was imbued with a spirit of pragmatic innovation, and he specifically refused to be bound by any system of a priori absolutes:

The first step must be to rid our minds of the idea that there are any such things in social matters as abstract rights, absolute principles, indefeasible laws, inalterable rules, or anything whatever of an external and inflexible nature.[30]

Whatever the difficulties with Jevons' system, Chamberlain relied upon its author's authority to justify state interference in place of laissez-faire. In a passage immediately following the one which Chamberlain quoted, Jevons formally attacked the doctrine

28. Parliamentary Debates, Fourth Series, 2, 1590.
29. W. Stanley Jevons, *The State in Relation to Labour* (London, Macmillan, 1883), p. 13. The passage has been misquoted (probably the error lies with the reporter of the debates, not Chamberlain) and reads as follows: "I conceive that the State is justified in passing any law, or even in doing any single act which, without ulterior consequences, adds to the sum total of happiness. Good done is sufficient justification of any act, in the absence of evidence that equal or greater evil will subsequently follow."
30. Ibid., p. 6.

of laissez-faire: "The liberty of the subject is only the means towards an end; it is not itself the end; hence, when it fails to produce the desired end, it may be set aside, and other means employed." The author of course refers to the "liberty" implicit in a laissez-faire system. It is this "liberty" that may be set aside in favor of state interference in the event the desired good fails to occur. Certainly when palpable evil results from the laissez-faire system the state should resort to interference. In order to determine the best course of action, Jevons recommended that the state use the experimental method: in the usual absence of certain evidence as to how to remedy a particular evil, Parliament must observe it closely, propose a remedy, try it out, and if it works, keep it. "Such special legislation no doubt needs to be watched, but when properly watched presents the *best* method of gaining experience. It amounts, in fact, to experimental legislation."[31]

Chamberlain, largely a self-educated man, read voraciously all his life. He certainly was familiar with Jevons' writing; whether Jevons influenced his thinking, or whether Chamberlain merely resorted to Jevons for independent corroboration of his already formed beliefs, will remain largely an academic question. Certain it is that Chamberlain acted in accordance with his stated beliefs, and supported those beliefs with quotations drawn from Jevons' writing. Chamberlain's willingness to countenance "experimental legislation" should already be apparent from his proposed amendment to the second reading of the 1893 Employers' Liability Bill. He carried this willingness into effect with his Workmen's Compensation Act of 1897, for that Act amounted to purely experimental legislation in a wholly untried direction.

When Salisbury took over the Prime Ministership in August 1895, he commanded a Government which was probably the most powerful of the century. That Government had committed itself absolutely to passing a Workmen's Compensation Bill along the lines suggested by Chamberlain in 1893 and promised by him in

31. W. Stanley Jevons, *Methods of Social Reform* (London, Macmillan, 1883), p. 261.

his campaign speeches of 1894. Salisbury had expressed entire willingness to support Chamberlain's ideas, both in his speech in the House of Lords and in his acceptance of the proposals contained in Chamberlain's "Memorandum of a Program of Social Reform." But one further consideration rendered Chamberlain's proposal the only possible solution: an Employers' Liability Bill no longer constituted an acceptable alternative. The moment the Liberals should finally pull themselves together and return to power, they would simply repeal the clause permitting contracting out, a clause to which the Conservatives had unequivocally committed themselves and which they would have to include in any future Employers' Liability Bill.

Since the will and the power to pass a Workmen's Compensation Act were present in Salisbury's third Government, the actual details of the passage are of little moment. The Government did not introduce any legislation on the subject during either the balance of 1895 or 1896, being occupied with other more pressing affairs. On 20 November 1896 Arthur Forwood introduced a private bill, which carried the backing of Chamberlain, along substantially the lines subsequently adopted by the Government; the bill was dropped upon receipt of assurance that the Government intended to introduce its own bill during the course of the 1897 session.[32]

On 3 May 1897, Matthew White Ridley (the Home Secretary) introduced the Government's Workmen's Compensation Bill in the House of Commons. As well as his own, the bill bore the name of the Attorney General and Joseph Chamberlain. In introducing the bill, Ridley touched upon the objection outlined above to another Employers' Liability Act:

> It seemed to us that we had two alternatives before us—one the alternative of adopting something like the provision of my right honorable friend opposite [Asquith], adding to it,

as we were pledged to do, the power of contracting out (or
as I would prefer to put it, giving the power to employers
and employed to contract themselves under proper safeguards
into a better position). The other alternative we had was to
propose a scheme of general compensation.[33]

He went on to announce that the Government had rejected the
first alternative in favor of the second.

Cleverly, Ridley made use of Asquith's own words to argue
for the proposed bill. Recalling the debate on the second reading
of the Employers' Liability Act of 1893, Ridley stated that the
Workmen's Compensation Bill

proceeds on the principle which I will venture to quote from
the words used by my right honorable friend opposite in
1893, that, "when a person, on his own responsibility and for
his own profit, sets in motion agencies which create risks for
others, he ought to be civilly responsible for the consequences
of what he does." In our Bill we accept the principle laid
down by the right honorable Gentleman, and we accordingly
propose in the first clause that—
    "If in any employment to which this Act applies personal
injury by accident arising out of and in the course of the employment is caused to a workman, his employer shall, subject as hereinafter mentioned, be liable to pay compensation
in accordance with the First Schedule of this Act."[34]

Having thus established that the Government bill of 1897 proceeded on the same theory as that of the Liberal bill of 1893,
Ridley effectively precluded any opposition to the Workmen's
Compensation Act. Opposition in any case would have been futile,
since the Government had decided upon having the bill, and they
were bound to get precisely what they wanted because of their
overwhelming control of the House of Commons.

33. Parliamentary Debates, Fourth Series, *48*, 1426.
34. Ibid., p. 1427.

Asquith rose to speak immediately after Ridley. He announced that he would not oppose the bill but instead would try to extend its provisions to workers not included, specifically seamen, domestics, and agricultural workers. Several months later, during the brief debate on the third reading, Asquith again complained about the failure of the bill to include all classes of workers.[35] In view of his previous opposition to any measure which gave special privileges to any group, his position was entirely in keeping with his principles.

Asquith's speech upon the introduction of the bill set the tone for the entire debate: scarcely a single voice was raised in opposition; the Government was obliged to refuse amendment after amendment seeking to extend the provisions of the bill. With increasing exasperation Chamberlain asked for cooperation in getting the bill through, not swamping it with time-consuming amendments:

> If we are to be continually applying to the Bill new structures, the Bill itself (which is admitted to be one of the most important Bills that have been brought before the House in the last few years, which is admitted to be a revolutionary Bill) that Bill, I say, will certainly not get through the present session.[36]

Having spent two days on the second reading debate, ten days in Committee, and five days on consideration as amended in Committee, the House of Commons passed the third reading without a division on the 15th of July. The House of Lords received it the following day, devoted a total of three days to it and passed the third reading on the bill on 29 July. In the House of Lords the proceedings were enlivened only by the Earl of Wemyss who, being quite deaf, failed to understand that the third reading had already passed when he moved that consideration of the bill be

35. Ibid., *51*, 207.
36. Ibid., *49*, 1168.

put off for three months. After much shouting by the Earl of Kimberley, Wemyss was made to understand that he had missed his chance and that the bill was already on its way back to the House of Commons. There the Lords' amendments, which were of the most inconsequential nature, were speedily agreed to. The Workmen's Compensation Act received the Royal assent on the 6th of August 1897.

Small wonder, then, that such a "revolutionary" bill attracted so little attention. The thorny problem of what to do about the victims of industrial accidents had been so long before the public eye that when the solution finally became assured in the election of 1895, the nation figuratively heaved a sigh of relief and directed its attention elsewhere. That the solution hit upon was revolutionary is beyond dispute: from the point of view of the worker, he received a legal right to compensation at no expense to himself; from the point of view of the employer, the cost of accidents was to be computed as another cost of production in the same way as depreciation of capital assets; from the point of view of the common law, strict liability (liability without any imputation of fault) had been written into a statute.

Fundamentally the bill went unopposed by the employers, who had grown accustomed to the idea of having their liabilities extended in any event, because the cost of workmen's compensation based on a fixed schedule could be calculated; the cost of an unlimited Employers' Liability Bill might be ruinous. And it was supposed—wrongly in the event—that the Workmen's Compensation Act would put an end to the hated litigation inherent in any extended system of employers' liability. Strangely enough, the Trades Union Congress gave only lukewarm support to the bill; while in favor on principle, they let it be known that they did not consider it a substitute for the measure proposed by Asquith. Such an attitude leads one to suspect petulance at not having proposed workmen's compensation in the first place themselves. In any event they did not oppose the bill, and subsequently they contented themselves with agitating for its extension.

While one may easily read too much significance into any historical event, the failure of the Employers' Liability Bill in 1893 and the passage of the Workmen's Compensation Act in 1897 mark some sort of historical watershed. In a certain sense the proponents of both solutions aimed at the same end: they intended to provide relief for the victims of industrial accidents, and they intended to make the employer the vehicle for that relief. But the means by which the two bills proposed to accomplish those ends bore little resemblance to one another. Asquith intended to remove what he considered to be a defect in the common law. For him the doctrine of common employment amounted to an anomalous exception and a stumbling block in the path of the plaintiff. In removing it, he would be doing no more than "hindering a hindrance," and in advocating such a measure he was merely following the precepts of his old tutor, T. H. Green, and clearing the path for self-help. Above all Asquith opposed contracting out because such contracts required state supervision, and such supervision granted preferential treatment to one segment of the people.

Chamberlain proposed nothing so subtle as a change in the common law; having observed an obvious evil he set about correcting it in the most straightforward manner possible. Believing with W. Stanley Jevons that the state is justified in passing any law which adds to the sum total of happiness, he saw no objection to granting a right to compensation to workmen; he could see no harmful ulterior consequences in passing the ultimate cost of this compensation on to the consumer; and he most certainly was not hampered by any doctrinal beliefs in laissez-faire. If he relied on any doctrine he relied on the one included in his "Ransom" speech: "There is a doctrine in many men's mouths and in a few men's practice that property has obligations as well as rights." And Chamberlain was willing to enforce those obligations.

But finally, such theoretical and personal considerations can be

given too much weight. A real, if still limited, democracy had
arrived in England with the Reform Bill of 1884. That democracy
made its opinion felt by overwhelmingly electing the political
party which, among other things, had promised to enact a system
of workmen's compensation. The people were tired of ineffective
government. Perhaps here lies the real watershed.

APPENDIXES

APPENDIX I

EMPLOYERS' LIABILITY ACT, 1880*

ARRANGEMENT OF SECTIONS

Sections.

1. Amendment of law.
2. Exceptions to amendment of law.
3. Limit of sum recoverable as compensation.
4. Limit of time for recovery of compensation.
5. Money payable under penalty to be deducted from compensation under Act.
6. Trial of actions.
7. Mode of serving notice of injury.
8. Definitions.
9. Commencement of Act.
10. Short title.

An Act to extend and regulate the Liability of Employers to make Compensation for Personal Injuries suffered by Workmen in their service.—September 7th, 1880.

"Be it enacted by the Queen's most Excellent Majesty, by and with the advice and consent of the Lords Spiritual and Temporal, and Commons, in this present Parliament assembled, and by the authority of the same, as follows:—

"1. Where after the commencement of this Act personal injury is caused to a workman   *Amendment of law.*
"(1.) By reason of any defect in the condition of the ways, works, machinery, or plant connected with or used in the business of the employer; or
"(2.) By reason of the negligence of any person in the service of the employer who has any superintendence entrusted to him whilst in the exercise of such superintendence; or

*Employers' Liability Act of 1880, 43 and 44 Vict., ch. 42.

"(3.) By reason of the negligence of any person in the service of the employer to whose orders or directions the workman at the time of the injury was bound to conform, and did conform, where such injury resulted from his having so conformed; or

"(4.) By reason of the act or omission of any person in the service of the employer done or made in obedience to the rules or bye-laws of the employer, or in obedience to particular instructions given by any person delegated with the authority of the employer in that behalf; or

"(5.) By reason of the negligence of any person in the service of the employer who has the charge or control of any signal, points, locomotive engine, or train upon a railway, the workmen, or in case the injury results in death, the legal personal representatives of the workman, and any persons entitled in case of death, shall have the same right of compensation and remedies against the employer as if the workman had not been a workman of nor in the service of the employer, nor engaged in his work.

Exceptions
to amend-
ment of law.

"2. A workman shall not be entitled under this Act to any right of compensation or remedy against the employer in any of the following cases; that is to say,

"(1.) Under Sub-section 1 of Section 1, unless the defect therein mentioned arose from, or had not been discovered or remedied owing to the negligence of the employer, or of some person in the service of the employer, and entrusted by him with the duty of seeing that the ways, works, machinery, or plant were in proper condition.

"(2.) Under Sub-section 4 of Section 1, unless the injury resulted from some impropriety or defect in the rules, by-laws, or instructions therein mentioned; provided that where a rule or bye-law has been approved or has been accepted as a proper rule or bye-law by one of Her Majesty's Principal Secretaries of State, or by the Board of Trade or any other department of the Government, under or by virtue of any Act of Parliament, it shall not be deemed for the purposes of this Act to be an improper or defective rule or bye-law.

"(3.) In any case where the workman knew of the defect or negligence which caused his injury, and failed within a reasonable time to give, or cause to be given, information thereof to the employer or some person superior to himself in the service of the employer unless he was aware that the employer or such superior already knew of the said defect or negligence.

"3. The amount of compensation recoverable under this Act shall not exceed such sum as may be found to be equivalent to the estimated earnings, during the three years preceding the injury, of a person in the same grade employed during those years in the like employment and in the district in which the workman is employed at the time of the injury.

Limit of sum recoverable as compensation.

"4. An action for the recovery under this Act of compensation for an injury shall not be maintainable unless notice that injury has been sustained is given within six weeks, and the action is commenced within six months from the occurrence of the accident causing the injury, or, in case of death, within twelve months from the time of death: Provided always, that in case of death the want of such notice shall be no bar to the maintenance of such action if the judge shall be of opinion that there was reasonable excuse for such want of notice.

Limit of time for recovery of compensation.

"5. There shall be deducted from any compensation awarded to any workman, or representatives of a workman, or persons claiming by, under, or through a workman in respect of any cause of action arising under this Act, any penalty or part of a penalty which may have been paid in pursuance of any other Act of Parliament to such workman, representatives, or persons in respect of the same cause of action; and where an action has been brought under this Act by any workman, or the representatives of any workman, or any persons claiming by, under, or through such workman, for compensation in respect of any cause of action arising under this Act, and payment has not previously been made of any penalty or part of a penalty under any other Act of Parliament in respect of the same cause of action, such workman, representatives, or person shall not be entitled thereafter to receive any penalty or part of a penalty under any other Act of Parliament in respect of the same cause of action.

Money payable under penalty to be deducted from compensation under Act.

"6.—(1.) Every action for recovery of compensation under this Act shall be brought in a county court, but may, upon the

Trial of actions.

application of either plaintiff or defendant, be removed into a superior court in like manner and upon the same conditions as an action commenced in a county court may by law be removed.

"(2.) Upon the trial of any such action in a county court before the judge without a jury one or more assessors may be appointed for the purpose of ascertaining the amount of compensation.

"(3.) For the purpose of regulating the conditions and mode of appointment and remuneration of such assessors, and all matters of procedure relating to their duties, and also for the purpose of consolidating any actions under this Act in a county court, and otherwise preventing multiplicity of such actions, rules and regulations may be made, varied, and repealed from time to time in the same manner as rules and regulations for regulating the practice and procedure in other actions in county courts.

" 'County Court' shall, with respect to Scotland, mean the 'Sheriff's Court,' and shall, with respect to Ireland, mean the 'Civil Bill Court.'

"In Scotland any action under this Act may be removed to the Court of Session at the instance of either party, in the manner provided by, and subject to the conditions prescribed by, Section 9 of the Sheriff Courts (Scotland) Act, 1877.

"In Scotland the Sheriff may conjoin actions arising out of the same occurrence or cause of action, though at the instance of the different parties and in respect of different injuries.

"7. Notice in respect of an injury under this Act shall give the name and address of the person injured, and shall state in ordinary language the cause of the injury and the date at which it was sustained, and shall be served on the employer, or, if there is more than one employer, upon one of such employers.

"The notice may be served by delivering the same to or at the residence or place of business of the person on whom it is to be served.

"The notice may also be served by post by a registered letter addressed to the person on whom it is to be served at his last known place of residence or place of business; and, if served by post, shall be deemed to have been served at the time when a letter containing the same would be delivered in the ordinary course of post; and, in proving the service of such notice, it shall

40 & 41
Vict. c. 50.

Mode of
serving
notice of
injury.

be sufficient to prove that the notice was properly addressed and registered.

"Where the employer is a body of persons corporate or unincorporate, the notice shall be served by delivering the same at or by sending it by post in a registered letter addressed to the office, or, if there be more than one office, any one of the offices of such body.

"A notice under this Section shall not be deemed invalid by reason of any defect or inaccuracy therein, unless the judge who tries the action arising from the injury mentioned in the notice shall be of opinion that the defendant in the action is prejudiced in his defence by such defect or inaccuracy, and that the defect or inaccuracy was for the purpose of misleading.

"8. For the purposes of this Act, unless the context otherwise requires,— **Definitions.**

"The expression 'person who has superintendence entrusted to him' means a person whose sole or principal duty is that of superintendence, and who is not ordinarily engaged in manual labour:

"The expression 'employer' includes a body of persons corporate or unincorporate: **38 & 39 Vict. c. 90.**

"The expression 'workman' means a railway servant and any person to whom the Employers and Workmen Act, 1875, applies. **Commencement of Act.**

"9. This Act shall not come into operation until the first day of January, one thousand eight hundred and eighty-one, which date is in this Act referred to as the commencement of this Act.

"10. This Act may be cited as the Employers' Liability Act, **Short title.** 1880, and shall continue in force till the thirty-first day of December one thousand eight hundred and eighty-seven, and to the end of the then next Session of Parliament, and no longer, unless Parliament shall otherwise determine, and all actions commenced under this Act before that period shall be continued as if the said Act had not expired."

APPENDIX II

(Excerpts from Public Record Office document, H.O. 45/9866/B13816)

Resolutions Concerning Contracting Out Received at the Home Office from Associations of Workmen up to 15 December 1893

Name	AGAINST allowing Contracting Out	IN FAVOR of Contracting Out
Trades Councils	27	0
Amalgamated Society of Railway Servants	99	0
Gas Workers Union	11	0
Other Trades Unions	17	0
Delegations of employees from L&NWRR	0	6
Other Societies and Meetings	7	5
Total	161	11

Bibliography

The documents referred to by the abbreviation "PRO" were photographed at the Public Record Office, London, during the summer of 1965. The documents were made available to the public only in 1957; as the seals on the cartons had not been disturbed when first examined by me, I assume that their contents have not been incorporated in any other study. Aside from the wealth of factual detail concerning the efforts of the Home Office to pass its various Employers' Liability Bills, I am indebted to the marginalia scribbled on the file folders for clues as to the emotional attitudes of the men directly involved in the struggle. While not cited in the book, those attitudes have colored my own on such issues as the role of labor unions and the feeling in the Government, after Gladstone resigned in 1894, toward the House of Lords. I can only hope that such feelings for the subject have not precluded an impartial attitude on my part.

For the rest, where possible, I have relied upon the most recent biographies for the history of the period and the personalities involved. Excepting only Chamberlain, every major figure has been the object of critical reevaluation by scholars during the last fifteen years. Strangely, Garvin's remains the only biography of Chamberlain of any consequence. Although Elsie Gulley was the first to pick up the influence of Jevons on Chamberlain, the significance escaped her entirely: she did no more than footnote the reference to his speech in the House of Commons. An alphabetical listing of the sources used follows.

Alderson, J. P., *Mr. Asquith,* London, Methuen, 1905.

Asquith, The Earl of Oxford and, *Memories and Reflections 1852–1927,* Boston, Little, Brown, 1928.

Baty, Thomas, *Vicarious Liability,* Oxford, Clarendon Press, 1916.

Baumann, A. A., *Persons and Politics of the Transition,* London, Macmillan, 1916.

Berlin, Sir Isaiah, *Two Concepts of Liberty,* Oxford, Clarendon Press, 1958.

Blackstone, Sir William, *Commentaries on the Laws of England,* W. D. Lewis, ed., Philadelphia, Rees Welsh, 1902, vol. 3.

Bosanquet, Bernard, *The Philosophical Theory of the State,* London, Macmillan, 1958.

Boyle, Sir Edward, ed., *Tory Democrat: Two Famous Disraeli Speeches,* London, Conservative Political Center, 1950.

Butler, Geoffrey G. *The Tory Tradition,* London, John Murray Publishers, 1914.

Cecil, Lady Gwendolen, *Life of Robert Marquis of Salisbury,* 4 vols., London, Hodder and Stoughton, 1921.

Churchill, W. S., *Lord Randolph Churchill,* 2 vols., New York, Macmillan, 1906.

Crewe, Lord, *Lord Rosebery,* London, Harper and Brothers, 1931.

Dicey, A. C., *Law and Public Opinion in England During the Nineteenth Century,* London, Macmillan, 1948.

Ensor, R. C. K., *England 1870–1914,* Oxford, Clarendon Press, 1936.

Evans, R. J., *The Victorian Age, 1815–1914,* London, Edward Arnold Publishers, 1950.

Fairfield, Charles, *A Memoir of Lord Bramwell,* London, Macmillan, 1898.

Fifoot, C. H. S., *Judge and Jurist in the Reign of Victoria,* London, Stevens, 1959.

Garvin, J. L., *The Life of Joseph Chamberlain,* 4 vols., London, Macmillan, 1932.

Green, T. H., *Liberal Legislation and Freedom of Contract,* Oxford, Slatter and Rose, 1881.

"Green, Thomas Hill," *Encyclopedia Britannica,* 11th ed. 12, 535.

Grisewood, Harman, ed., *Ideas and Beliefs of the Victorians,* London, Sylvan Press, 1949.

Gulley, Elsie E., *Joseph Chamberlain and English Social Politics,* New York, Columbia University Press, 1926.

Heuston, R. F. V., *Salmond on the Law of Torts,* 14th ed., London, Sweet and Maxwell, 1965.

James, Robert Rhodes, *Rosebery,* London, Weidenfeld and Nicolson, 1963.

Jenkins, Roy, *Asquith,* London, Collins, 1964.

Jevons, W. Stanley, *Methods of Social Reform,* London, Macmillan, 1883.

Jevons, W. Stanley, *The Theory of Political Economy*, New York, Sentry Press, 1965.

Kennedy, A. L., *Salisbury 1830–1903, Portrait of a Statesman*, London, John Murray, 1953.

Maccoby, S., *English Radicalism 1886–1914*, London, George Allen and Unwin, 1953.

Magnus, Philip, *Gladstone: A Biography*, New York, E. P. Dutton, 1954.

Marriott, Sir J. A. R., *Modern England, 1885–1932*, London, Methuen, 1934.

Morley, John, *The Life of William Ewart Gladstone*, 3 vols. in 2, London, Macmillan, 1911.

Morton, E. E., ed., *The Pocket Asquith*, London, Mills and Boon, 1914.

Parliamentary Debates, Third and Fourth Series (separate volumes cited in footnotes).

Raymond, E. T., *The Life of Lord Rosebery*, New York, George Doran, 1923.

Richter, Melvin, *The Politics of Conscience; T. H. Green and His Age*, Cambridge, Harvard University Press, 1964.

Ritchie, David G., *The Principles of State Interference*, London, Swan Sonnenschein, 1891.

Rosebery, Lord, *Lord Randolph Churchill*, New York and London, Harper and Brothers, 1906.

Ruegg, A. H., *The Laws Regulating the Relation of Employer and Workman in England*, London, William Clowes and Sons, 1905.

Spender, J. A., and Asquith, Cyril, *Life of Herbert Henry Asquith, Lord Oxford and Asquith*, 2 vols. London, Hutchinson, 1932.

Webb, Sidney and Beatrice, *The History of Trade Unionism*, London, Longmans Green, 1935.

Whates, H., *The Third Salisbury Administration*, London, Vacher and Sons, 1900.

Wilkinson, William J., *Tory Democracy*, New York, Columbia University Press, 1925.

Wilson, Sir Arnold, and Levy, Hermann, *Workmen's Compensation*, 2 vols. London, Oxford University Press, 1939.

Young, A. F., *Industrial Injuries Insurance*, London, Routledge and Kegan Paul, 1964.

Index

Abinger, Lord, 11–12

Accident prevention legislation, 5, 25, 36, 62, 64, 83, 87, 104–05. *See also bills and acts by name*

Agricultural depression *(1879–86)*, 42

Argyll, Duke of, 78

Asquith, Cyril, 51

Asquith, Herbert Henry, 91, 101, 104; biographical note, 47–49; support of Employers' Liability Act *(1890)*, 39–40; preparation and support of Employers' Liability Bill *(1893)*, 39, 57–61, 63–64, 65, 71–72, 75–76, 79, 84–86; on contracting out, 40, 60, 65–76, 84, 86, 105; admiration for William Gladstone, 48–49; Benjamin Jowett's influence on, 50–51, 64; T. H. Green's influence on, 51–56, 105; on government interference, 57, 64, 105; on vicarious liability, 59; on doctrine of common employment, 59–60, 65–67, 85–86, 105; conflict with Joseph Chamberlain, 63, 76; on industrial insurance, 63–64; and London and North Western Railway case, 68–70; on Trades Dispute Bill *(1906)*, 84–85; on Workmen's Compensation Act *(1897)*, 102, 103; on laissez-faire, 105

Balfour, Arthur James, 31, 33

Balliol College (Oxford University), 49 ff.

Baty, Thomas, 8, 9

Beaconsfield, Earl of. *See* Disraeli, Benjamin

Berlin, Sir Isaiah, 53–54

Blackburn, Justice, 8

Blackstone, Sir William, 6, 7

Board of Trade, administrative role of, 65, 74, 77, 78

Bosanquet, Bernard, 56

Bramwell, Lord, 13

Brassey, Sir Thomas, 19, 34–35

Bright, John, 52

Broadhurst, Henry, 60; on contracting out, 33–34, 37; appointed President of Board of Trade, 34; Bills of *1887* and *1888*, 37

Burt, E. A. 60; on contracting out, 33–34, 37; Bills of *1887* and *1888*, 37; association with Employers' Liability Bill *(1891)*, 37, 40; association with Employers' Liability Bill *(1893)*, 57

Campbell-Bannerman, Sir Henry, 84–85

Cecil, Robert (Marquis of Salisbury), 72; biographical note, 93–96; and Joseph Chamberlain, 27, 31–33, 57, 91–93, 96, 100–01; second Government of, 30, 31, 37; and Lord Randolph Churchill, 31–33; on Home Rule, 32–33, 47, 82; on Employers' Liability Bill *(1893)*, 78, 81, 82, 83, 91–92; leads Unionist Government, 89, 92, 100; on workmen's insurance funds, 91; supports Workmen's Compensation Act *(1897)*, 93, 100–01; on Reform Bill *(1867)*, 93–94; and Benjamin Disraeli, 93–95

Celtic Fringe, 46, 83

Chamberlain, Joseph, 39, 46, 71, 86; biographical note, 96–98; cited, 5; and Employers' Liability Act *(1880)*, 19; leads Radical Wing of

Liberal Party, 26–29; influence of
Henry George on, 27; on Reform
Bill *(1884)*, 27; and Marquis of
Salisbury, 27, 31–33, 57, 91–93,
96, 100–01; "Unauthorized Program" of, 27–29, 33, 34; "Ransom"
speech of, 28, 105; Preface to *The
Radical Program*, 29; and Home
Rule, 29, 30, 72; conflict with William Gladstone, 29–31, 44–45, 97–
98; leaves Liberal Party, 29–31, 48;
and Lord Randolph Churchill, 31–
32, 57; on Unionist alliance, 32–
33; Benjamin Disraeli's influence
on, 44–45; leads Radical Conservatives, 57, 81; on workmen's compensation, 61, 87, 90–91, 103; on
Employers' Liability Bill *(1893)*,
61–65, 75–76, 79–81, 82, 83, 87,
91–92, 100, 101; on moral liability,
62–63; confrontation with Herbert
Asquith, 63–64, 75–76, 79–80;
"Memorandum of a Program of
Social Reform," 91; leads Unionist
Government, 92; directorship of
Nettleford and Chamberlain, 97;
on laissez-faire, 97–100; on Eight-
Hour Bill, 98–99; influence of W.
Stanley Jevons on, 98–100, 105

Churchill, Lord Randolph, 98; and
Employers' Liability Bill *(1880)*,
19; leader of Fourth Party, 19, 31;
opposes William Gladstone, 31,
44–45; and Joseph Chamberlain,
31–32, 57; and Lord Salisbury,
31–33; for Unionist alliance, 32; on
Home Rule, 32–33; leader of Radical Conservatives, 57

Churchill, Winston, on Lord Rosebery, 88–89

Cobb, H. T., 69, 74

Collectivism: William Gladstone on,
45; T. H. Green on, 52, 54; Arnold
Toynbee on, 55; Beatrice Webb on,
55

Common employment: origin and
definition, 11; and vicarious liability, 12–13; Lord Bramwell on,
13; objections to, 13–14, 15; Parliamentary discussion and limitations of, 15–16, 18–19, 40, 77;
Royal Commission on Railways on,
17; Employers' Liability Act *(1880)*
on, 20–21; abolition of, 25, 37,
58, 85; Employers' Liability Bill
(1891) on, 37; miners on, 40; defence of, 40, 60, 105; Employers'
Liability Bill *(1893)* on, 58, 83, 85;
Herbert Asquith on, 60–61, 65–67,
85

Conservatives: on Home Rule, 30, 33,
90; alliance with Liberal Unionists,
30–33, 48, 81–83, 90; and employers' liability legislation, 33, 57, 81,
90, 92; Radical Wing leadership of,
57; on contracting out, 68; control
of Government, 83; *1895*, victory,
92

Contracting out, 101–02; explanation
of, 23–24; *Griffiths v. Earl of
Dudley* decision on, 24, 33; labor
union opposition to, 33, 34, 40, 67,
74, 75, 77, 83; Liberty and Property Defense League on, 34; Employers' Liability Bills legislation
on, 35–39, 58, 65–67, 70–73, 74–
76, 82, 83; Herbert Asquith on, 40,
60, 65–76, 84, 86, 105; Joseph
Chamberlain on, 65; House of
Lords discussion on, 67–68, 76–78,
80, 82; London and North Western
Railway Company on, 68–70, 73;
William Johnson on, 72; amendment provisions for, 74, 76–78;
Earl of Dudley on, 77–78; William
Gladstone on, 81; T. H. Green on,
86

Contractors, liability of, 36, 40

Cross, Sir R. A., 17

Demonstrations of the unemployed, 42

Dilke, Sir Charles, 26

Disraeli, Benjamin, 15; Government bill on doctrine of common employment, 18; Government of dismissed, 18; on Employers' Liability Act (*1880*), 19; disagreement with William Gladstone, 44–45; and Joseph Chamberlain, 44–45; and Lord Randolph Churchill, 44–45, 98; disagreement with Lord Salisbury, 93–95; on social reform, 93, 94–95, 98

Dudley Amendment, 77–78, 79, 80–81, 82; Herbert Asquith on, 86

Dudley, Earl of, 77–78, 83. *See also* Dudley Amendment; *Griffiths v. Earl of Dudley*

Eight-Hour Bill, 45–46, 98

Employers' liability: and rule of vicarious liability, 8–10; as campaign issue, 18, 57, 83, 90; extension of, 22, 37–38, 61–63, 83, 104; legislation, 33, 37–40, 60, 90; Sir Godfrey Lushington on, 39–40; Newcastle Program on, 46; Herbert Asquith on, 59–61; Joseph Chamberlain on, 61–63, 65. *See also bills and acts by name*

Employers' Liability Act (*1880*), 6, 86, 109–13; Fourth Party criticism of, 19; passage and amendment of, 19; provisions and interpretation of, 20–22; recovery of damages under, 22, 24–25; effect on Friendly Societies, 22–24, 25; effect on contracting out, 23–24; failures of, 25–26, 35; influence on future legislation, 33–37, 39, 75

Employers' Liability Bill (*1888*), 37–38

Employers' Liability Bill (*1890*), 38–39, 40, 66

Employers' Liability Bill (*1891*), 37, 39

Employers' Liability Bill (*1893*), 5, 39, 56; Herbert Asquith on, 39, 57, 59–61, 63–64, 65, 72, 75–76, 79, 84–86; introduction of, 57–59; second reading, 59–65; Joseph Chamberlain on, 61–65, 75–76, 79–83, 87, 100, 101; Parliamentary discussion and amendments, 67–68, 70–81; railway reaction to, 68–70, 71; effect of Home Rule Bill on, 72; Lord Salisbury on, 78, 81, 82, 83, 91–92; failure of, 81–82, 105; analysis of action on, 83–86; influence on Workmen's Compensation Act (*1897*), 102, 105

Factory Acts, 5, 58–59

Fourth Party, 19, 31

Friendly Societies, 77; development and function of, 22–23, 25; effect of contracting out on, 24, 36, 70, 75–76; employers' contributions to, 37, 58–59, 65, 66, 68, 71

Gladstone, Herbert (Attorney-General), 57, 73

Gladstone, William E., 19, 41, 78; Liberal Party leader (*1885*), 26; Home Rule Bills and policy of, 29–30, 44–45, 46–47, 57, 72; disagreement with Joseph Chamberlain, 29–31, 44–45, 97–98; Lord Randolph Churchill's criticism of, 31, 44–45; on contracting out, 34, 81; association with Manchester School philosophy, 44–45; disagreement with Benjamin Disraeli, 44–45; on Eight-Hour Bill, 45–46; on Newcastle Program, 46, 57; attack on House of Lords, 47, 81–84, 87; influence on Herbert Asquith, 48, 49, 64; and Employers' Liability Bill (*1893*), 81–84

Gorst, John 31
Green, T. H.: influence on Herbert
Asquith, 51–52, 56, 57, 64, 85–
86, 105; political and ethical philosophy of, 51–55, 85, 86; influence
on Arnold Toynbee, 55–56
Griffiths v. Earl of Dudley (1881), 24,
33, 77

Harcourt, Sir William, 92
Home Rule. *See* Ireland, Home Rule
for
Home Rule Bill (1886), Parliamentary action on, 29–30
Home Rule Bill *(1893)*, Parliamentary action on, 47, 57, 72, 82, 84

Insurance funds. *See* Workmen's in-
surance funds
Ireland, Home Rule for: Joseph
Chamberlain leaves Liberal Party
over, 29–30; William Gladstone
on, 29–30, 32, 44–47, 57, 72; Lord
Salisbury on, 32; Lord Randolph
Churchill on, 32; affects Unionist
alliance and victory, 32, 78, 89–90,
92; Lord Rosebery on, 89. *See also*
Home Rule Bill *(1886)*; Home
Rule Bill *(1893)*

James, Sir Henry, 19, 90–91
Jevons, W. Stanley, influence of political philosophy on Joseph Chamberlain, 98–100, 105
Jowett, Benjamin, influence on Herbert Asquith, 50–51, 64

Kant, Immanuel, 52–53
Kimberley, Lord, 30, 104

Labor unions, on contracting out, 33,
73–74, 83, 115. *See also* Trades
unions
Laissez-faire: Joseph Chamberlain's
opposition to, 29, 97–100, 105;
Manchester School's support of, 44–

46, 97; William Gladstone's support of, 45; T. H. Green on, 51–53
Laski, H. J., 51, 56
Law Reform (Personal Injuries) Act
(1948), 12, 25
Levy, Hermann (Professor), 12
Liberal Caucus *(1891)*, 46–47
Liberal Nonconformists, 96
Liberals: *1880* campaign issue of, 19;
radical reform movement among,
26, 29, 31, 55–56, 89; on Home
Rule Bill *(1886)*, 30; adopt New-
castle Program *(1891)*, 46, 57, 89;
collapse of *(1895)*, 87–89, 92. *See
also* Liberal Unionists
Liberal Unionists, alliance with Con-
servatives, 30–33, 48, 81–83, 90
Liberty and Property Defense League,
34
*Limpus v. London General Omnibus
Company*, and vicarious liability,
8–10
London and North Western Insurance
Society, 72 f.
London and North Western Railway
Company case, 78; and Friendly
Society membership requirement,
68–70; on contracting out, 68–74,
115; H. T. Cobb on, 69; effect on
Employers' Liability Bill *(1893)*,
74
London Dockers' Strike *(1889)*, 43
Lowe, Mr. (Lord Sherbrooke), recom-
mendation on doctrine of common
employment, 16
Lushington, Sir Godfrey, 39–40

MacDonald, Alexander: doctrine of
common employment bill, 15, 17;
on contracting out, 33; and Irish
Phoenix Park murders case, 49
Maclaren Amendment (contracting-
out, 71, 74–75
Manchester School, 54; philosophy of,
44–45, 52, 97

Matthews, Henry, 37–38, 74
Miners, voice in reform legislation, 34, 40–41, 67, 98
Miners' Federation of Great Britain, The, 43, 79; on Employers' Liability Act (*1890*), 40–41; on contracting out, 67
Miners' Permanent Relief Society, 78 f.
Morley, John, 92, 97

National Liberal Federation, 48
Negligence, 17; origin and definition, 6–7; and rule of vicarious liability, 9–11, 36, 59; contributory, 10, 61; and defense of common employment, 11–16; and rule of *Volenti non fit injuria*, 13; under Employers' Liability Act (*1880*), 20–21, 25; Friendly Societies' view of, 22; and contracting out, 24, 67; under Employers' Liability Bill (*1893*), 58–61
Newcastle Program, 57, 89–90; articles of, 46
New Unionism, 43, 67
Northcote, Sir Stafford, 31

Oldbury Alkali Company, 76 f.

Parnell, Charles Stewart, 29, 30; and Phoenix Park murders, 48–49
Partisanship of House of Lords, 47, 82–83, 87
Paternal government, principle of, 53, 64
Phoenix Park murders, 48–49
Pigott, Richard, 48–49
Priestley v. Fowler (1837), 11
Principal Secretaries, administrative role, 65
Public Health Act (*1875*), 94

Railway servants, 17, 67; Amalgamated Society of Railway Servants, 70, 115

Reform Bill (*1867*), Lord Salisbury on, 93–94
Reform Bill (*1868*), 97
Reform Bill (*1884*), 106; enfranchised voters under, 27–28, 34
Ridley, Matthew White, 72, 101–02
Ripon, Marquess of, 30, 77
Ritchie, David G., 56
Rosebery, Lord, 30; heads Liberal Government, 87–89, 92; contempt for Parliament, 88
Rothschild, Hanna, wife of Lord Rosebery, 88

Salisbury, Lord (Marquis of). *See* Cecil, Robert
Scotland. *See* Celtic Fringe
Second Home Rule Bill. *See* Home Rule Bill (*1893*)
Select Committee (House of Commons): on doctrine of common employment, 15–16, 18; examination of Employers' Liability Act (*1880*), 33–37
Sherbrooke, Lord. *See* Lowe, Mr.
Smith v. Charles Baker and Sons (1891), 22
Social Democratic Federation, 42
State interference: William Gladstone on, 44–45; Herbert Asquith on, 63–64; Joseph Chamberlain on, 98–100; W. Stanley Jevons on, 98–100
Stevedores' Union, 43
Strict liability, 7, 60–61, 104
Subcontractors, liability of, 36, 40

Toynbee, Arnold, 64; radicalism of, 55–56
Trade unionism, 64–65, 81
Trades Councils, 115
Trades Dispute Bill (*1906*), 84–85
Trades Union Congress, 64, 73, 104–05
Trades Union Council, 80

Trades unions, 43, 64–65, 68, 94, 115; opposition to Employers' Liability Bill *(1890)*, 40; on contracting out, 67, 75; Trades Dispute Bill *(1906)* on, 84–85. *See also* Labor unions

"Unauthorized Program" of Joseph Chamberlain, 27–29, 33, 34

Unionism. *See* New Unionism; Trade unionism

Unionists: alliance of, 26, 27, 32, 87, 89–90, 92; workmen's compensation legislation, 91–93, 102–04. *See also* Conservatives; Liberal Unionists

Vicarious liability: rule of, 8–12, 17–18; opposition to, 13–14; Herbert Asquith on, 59–61

Victoria, Queen, 6, 87 f.

Wales. *See* Celtic Fringe

Willes, Justice, decision on vicarious liability, 8–10

Workmen's compensation, 5–6, 22; under Employers' Liability Act *(1880)*, 35–37; under Employers' Liability Bill *(1893)*, 61–63, 71, 87; Joseph Chamberlain on, 61–63, 87, 90–91; unions on, 68; Earl of Dudley on, 78. *See also* Workmen's insurance funds

Workmen's Compensation Act *(1897)*, 22, 26, 71, 87; introduction and provisions, 5, 100–05; Lord Salisbury's support of, 93, 100–01

Workmen's insurance funds: Friendly Societies' management of, 22, 36; employers' contributions to, 22–23, 35–37, 38, 68–69, 74, 78; effect of contracting out on, 23–24, 36, 74; Herbert Asquith's objections to, 63–64; Lord Salisbury on, 91

DATE DUE

GAYLORD			PRINTED IN U.S.A.